AF571739

STRATEGIC PLANNING

GERALD L. GORDON

Library of Congress Cataloging-in-Publication Data

Gordon, Gerald L.
Strategic planning for association executives/Gerald L. Gordon.
-- 1st ed.
p. cm.
Includes bibliographical references
1. Trade associations -- United States -- Management. 2. Strategic planning. I. Title
HD2425.G67 1997
658.4 012--dc21 97-5285
CIP

Copyright © 1997 by the American Society of Association Executives, Publishers, 1575 Eye Street, NW, Washington, DC 20005. All rights reserved. No part of this book may be reproduced in any form, by any process or technique, without the express written consent of the publisher.

American Society of Association Executives
1575 Eye Street, NW
Washington, DC 20005-1168

Kudos for Strategic Planning:

"Dr. Gordon's work with the City of Poznan (Poland) confirmed that we were taking the correct steps in the planning of our future economy. We are confident that we have a clear vision of our opportunities and a plan to take our economy into the 21st century."

Lech Langowski, Director
Department of Information and Development
City of Poznan, Poland

"Your technique made it possible for each member to participate. As a result of the workshops, departments will be able to prepare their personal strategic plans which will ensure effectiveness and efficiency for the City of Dallas."

John L. Ware, City Manager
City of Dallas, Texas

"Gerry Gordon's gentle, but firm hand guided Leadership Fairfax, Incorporated's board of directors through the critical process of forming the first strategic plan for the organization. Gerry's insightful observations and humor helped us to stay focused and on target. We were able to discuss and reach consensus on potentially divisive issues without resentment or gridlock."

John E. Ritzert, Jr.
Ritzert & Leyton
Fairfax, Virginia

The author has worked to ensure that all information in this book is accurate as of the time of publication and consistent with standards of good practice in the general management community. As research and practice advance, however, standards may change. For this reason, it is recommended that readers evaluate the applicability of any recommendations in light of particular situations and changing standards.

Table of Contents

Introduction

Strategic planning is a process of controlling destiny rather than leaving it to random future events. By appraising future opportunities, as well as its own existing and future strengths and weaknesses, an association can help ensure its success and avoid identifiable problems. Following the lead of the business community, associations have come to embrace the concept of strategic planning over the past decade.

As distant countries and their markets have grown closer through technological advances, and as competition has changed, new opportunities have been created. But these new opportunities carry attendant risks. In the private sector, if companies are going to minimize the risks in attempting to maximize profits, they must establish formal planning systems to replace older, informal, intuitive methods. The business world has generally accepted this premise, and associations have followed suit, adapting strategic planning methods to their own needs.

As acceptance of strategic planning has grown, so has the body of literature that examines its various aspects and applications. These books and journals have proven useful. Business executives have learned the value of scrutinizing shifts in existing markets, the evolution of new markets, changes in the domestic economy and foreign markets, and other environmental factors that affect the ability of a corporation to achieve its goals and objectives.

The lion's share of research and scholarly thought has been devoted to the impact of planning on profit, market share, and return on investment. Yet the same environmental factors that affect a business' bottom line can also affect an organization's ability to be successful. It is this realization that has spurred trade and professional associations to undertake strategic planning.

This book addresses strategic planning in the context of trade and professional associations, whose primary orientation is not the bottom line, but providing service to its membership and other constituencies with finite resources and motives other than profit.

Despite this fundamental difference from a business, an association must have the same short-term and long-term orientation as a company. A business has short-term profit and market share targets; an association has short-term service provision goals. A business must plan for future growth in existing and new markets; an association must plan for future demands for public services with either a shrinking, a static, or an expanding pool of human and capital resources. In short, an association must satisfy today's needs for constituent services and seek the means of providing improved services in the years to come.

This is not to say that strategic planning is easy to implement. Taking a long term view may run counter to an association's need to concentrate more intensely on one- to two-year planning. To some extent, this choice is and must be driven by budgetary considerations. The ability of an association to provide member services depends on the availability of revenues and other resources necessary to support them. Membership revenues are not always easy to project far into the future. Planning helps an association to identify and mobilize its available resources and to apply them to the most pressing needs. Planning can also have tremendous value in bolstering members' confidence in the future. It will aid in the assessment of current practices, validate or refute currently held assumptions, facilitate networking between various groups in the field(s), and increase everyone's knowledge of and appreciation for professional staff, the group's leadership, and other volunteers.

Many associations have already recognized the value of strategic planning in the same way that many companies have. The American Association of Law Libraries in Chicago developed a plan in order to respond to several strategic directions that had been identified by a planning committee. AALL needed the process to:

- reinvigorate the structure of AALL
- provide leadership to shape the legal information environment in a time of rapid technological and public policy changes
- increase and diversify AALL's education offerings to members and non-members
- encourage and support strategic partnerships and purposeful exchanges with others
- create financial stability to support the program and membership through prudent use of resources
- build a superlative association and headquarters operation

As noted earlier, most of the literature on strategic planning focuses on the private sector; yet many of the lessons are applicable to strategic planning in the context of association management as well.

It is the intent of this book to draw these lessons from the private sector planning literature and to introduce some practical applications for associations in a format which can be used by association executives and volunteers as they work to anticipate the future and to develop strategies for maximizing opportunities and minimizing threats.

Like businesses, trade and professional associations must be responsive to changes in their environment. A business does so to determine how best to allocate personnel, equipment, and capital to maximize return on investment. An association must also allocate human and capital resources to its best advantage.

In order to provide other and more effective services, associations need to assess what the demands will be and the relative value of competing needs. All of this must be accomplished against an almost certain assumption: the sum of all valid needs will exceed the availability of resources. To compound this dilemma, the allocation of scarce resources is based on an imperfect understanding of future needs.

As the economy becomes more complex, the nature and the rapidity of change become more important in determining future member needs and in constraining the ability of associations to meet them. As the very nature of working changes, services must adapt. As the rate of technological change increases, organizations must respond more diligently. As state, federal, and local regulations come and go, entities must react. As the environment in which an organization must operate becomes more complex, its leadership must become more sensitive to those complexities and to the degree and types of change needed. In short, the staff and volunteers must have a realistic vision of the future, and strategies to pursue that vision.

Some associations have only recently begun to plan their futures in a conscious and systematic way. The absence of planning and its benefits is frequently noted by groups that are either initiating or reinstating a strategic planning process. Witness, for example, the following statement from the strategic plan of the National Court Reporters Association in Tysons Corner, Virginia: "In 1990-91, NCRA undertook its first strategic planning process in many years...as 1994 began, we were ready to resume the planning process...create vision of the future and what we as an organization need to do to make that future a reality. We proceeded with the belief that our planning must focus on meeting core member needs."

The benefits of strategic planning

To fully appreciate the benefits of strategic planning, it is useful to recognize its nature: it is both a process and a product. The process is a systematic examination of the organization and its environment by those who have a stake in its future success. The product is a document specifying the actions required to achieve future goals based on the information unearthed during the planning process. Together, these components of strategic planning yield numerous benefits to any organization.

Anticipation of the future First, strategic planning improves the odds that an organization will succeed in its mission by helping its leaders comprehend the future and the position of the organization within it rather than reacting to future events as they occur. Strategic planning is the anticipation of future problems and opportunities. If these are identified before they are encountered, they can be either minimized or maximized as appropriate. If they are not identified, opportunities can be missed and problems can grow to insurmountable proportions. For these reasons, many associations begin the planning process by identifying some general aims for the organizations in the future. Two such examples are illustrated in the box on this page.

Assessment of the organization Second, strategic planning forces people within an organization to come together to discuss the strengths and weaknesses of their organization, where they would like to go, and how best to get there.

Organizational goal setting and consensus building Third, strategic planning promotes goal-setting and reaching a consensus around those goals. This enhances the likelihood of achieving the goals. As will be discussed

General Aims (from the Strategic Plan of the Reston, Virginia-based Associated Landscape Contractors of America):

ALCA as an Industry Leader

By 1995, ALCA will be viewed as a spokesperson for the industry. In the field of education, it will be strongly influential in curriculum development at institutions of higher learning, and it will be seen as the prime guide regarding career opportunities in the green industry. It will be a clearinghouse for environmental updates. Related industries, institutions, and governmental agencies will look to ALCA for guidance and information regarding green industry questions. It will be a force for research and development. The media will seek its opinions regarding green industry issues

ALCA's Marketing Effort

By 1995, architects and designers will have ALCA's "Who's Who..." in their office. ALCA will be presenting a clear image to the marketplace. All of ALCA's publication or material will have a uniform quality look. Individuals and organizations desiring landscape services will seek out ALCA's members and know where to find them. ALCA will have a very high renewal rate. It will possess a substantial leadership pool. It will provide guidance to members on how to launch an effective marketing effort.

later, establishing goals for an organization requires the give-and-take of negotiation as participants seek ways to align organizational strengths with future opportunities and challenges.

This process tends to result in compromising on commonly accepted targets and programs. This process is particularly vital for an association because its programs may directly impact the ability of its membership to succeed in their individual business or other endeavors. Others may directly affect the success of the organization's very mission: educational, charitable, health research, or other. Due to the very criticality of the many purposes of associ-

Membership

By 1995, ALCA will be providing increased tangible benefits to its members. It will have developed a membership structure that will enable a large number of people to participate at an appropriate level of involvement to fit their professional and organizational needs. ALCA will have developed its monthly newsletter into a sophisticated magazine that will proclaim ALCA activities as well as individual member "Good News."

ALCA's Legislative Effort

By 1995, ALCA will be recognizing and monitoring emerging issues and developing position statements that will benefit its membership. ALCA will be in a proactive role alone or in conjunction with other groups and governmental agencies for determining future legislation.

Education

By 1995, ALCA will be recognized as the leader in providing educational opportunities that can best be provided by its national resource bank for its members through conferences, publications, videos, and new technology available in the marketplace. Education will be provided to all levels of ALCA's member organizations.

ations, it is important to use the planning process as a venue in which to bring disparate perspectives into the open, debate the relative merits of various issues and mixes of service and resource allocations, and arrive at acceptable compromises. Thus, strategic planning must frequently arrive at painful concessions or even outright disagreement or disapproval. This process may, however, be regarded as a strength, despite the degree of difficulty and consternation involved.

Allocation of resources Fourth, strategic planning facilitates the ever-difficult process of human and capital

Initial Objectives of the State Medical Society of Wisconsin (SMS):

1. Ensure that physicians are active players in decisions regarding patient care
2. Represent physician and patient goals to decision making bodies
3. Improve communication of the value of SMS membership to each member segment
4. Improve communication to member physicians in our three major spheres of activity (political, scientific, and socioeconomic)
5. Increase member approval rating...by making sure that SMS services and activities are aligned with member needs and interests
6. Evaluate the structure of SMS governance to ensure that it remains responsive and representative
7. Position SMS as the organization that efficiently determines the healthcare goals of physicians and patients
8. Maximize physician influence in the emerging integrated systems

resource allocation. All organizations have finite resources to allocate to their products, services, and functions. The allocation of scarce resources must consider all potential demands and the impact of providing one project, service, or function over another. In the corporate sector, these competing demands may be research and development, marketing, and capital investment in new plants. In the field of association management, the competing demands are all the services the organization provides as well as those for which provision is being sought.

Establishment of benchmarks Finally, strategic planning provides benchmarks. The goals and objectives define the direction from the beginning of a program or

9. Develop new ways for more members to participate in SMS activities
10. Interpret and facilitate the implementation of decisions made regarding physicians and patients
11. Increase resident and young physician involvement in SMS
12. Ensure appropriate physician security and just compensation
13. Maintain the Society's sound financial position by increased attention to cost-benefit analysis of services and activities
14. Penetrate hospital staff and large group staff meetings as an alternative conduit to county medical societies
15. Evaluate the status of unified counties with the State Medical Society
16. Be the identified source and controller of outcome data in Wisconsin

other fiscal or planning cycle. Subsequently, they provide the measurements against which performance can be gauged. Without goals and objectives, an organization cannot know whether it has been successful. Yet, as pointed out by the renowned strategist, Michael Kami, "Very few organizations can actually show you a concise strategic action plan." [1] Organizations would be well advised to heed the advice of the Mad Hatter, who explained to Alice in *Through the Looking Glass*, if you don't know "where you want to get to...it doesn't matter which way you go."

Associations that use strategic planning do so from a clear recognition of the needs for planning summarized above. So evident are these needs, in fact, that the plans often explicitly state the benefits expected to be derived. Such statements were made in the strategic plans of the Associated Landscape Contractors of America and the State Medical Society of Wisconsin, as shown in the sidebars on pages 6 through 9.

Preview of the book

This book outlines the strategic planning process for association executives and volunteers who seek to anticipate and shape the future of their organizations.

Associations conduct strategic planning exercises for different reasons. The impetus may be the need to increase revenues or member participation. It may reflect a periodic need to review programs and services. It may result from new or potential legislation that will have an impact upon the members' particular areas of interest. In some cases, it may simply be an effective means of managing the growth or decline of an industry or profession.

Planning may be driven by one key person to secure the benefits of a future opportunity, or it may be a practice commonly accepted as necessary for the proper management of change. In some groups, the process is a new one, while others communities are in their second or third generation of preparing plans.

Whatever prompts those affiliated with associations to engage in strategic planning, and at whatever evolutionary step the process is conducted, the process of planning and the structure of the plan itself will be very similar. This book will assist those involved in strategic planning.

The initial chapters of this book define the terms and describe the process. Subsequent chapters cite examples, real and fictitious, to demonstrate the principles involved. The final chapter provides a step-by-step strategic planning guide for associations and their executives, and extensive appendixes provide positive examples of written plans from a number of associations. A bibliography of related references is provided at the end of the book.

Excerpts from the strategic plans of numerous associations are used throughout this book to provide examples of alternative approaches and presentations. The willingness of these associations and their staffs to participate in this project is appreciated:

- The State Medical Society of Wisconsin
- The National Center for Teachers of Mathematics
- The Brick Institute of America
- Associated Landscape Contractors of America
- The Door and Hardware Institute
- The American Machine Tool Distributors Association
- The National Center for Missing and Exploited Children
- The Restaurant Association of Greater Washington
- The International Facilities Management Association
- The American Association of Law Libraries

- The Federation of American Societies for Experimental Biology
- The National Head Start Association
- The American Pharmaceutical Association
- The American Association of School Administrators
- The Printing Industries of America
- The American Consulting Engineers Council
- The National Court Reporters Association
- The Academy of General Dentistry
- The International Association of Financial Planners
- The Music Educators National Conference
- The Northern Virginia Technology Council
- The International Society of Optical Engineering
- The Professional Services Council
- The National Association of College Stores
- The American Roentgen Ray Society.

1. Michael Kami, Kami Strategic Assumptions (Lighthouse Point, FL: Kami, 1988), p.2.

Chapter I

What Is Strategic Planning?

Strategic planning in association management is a systematic process by which an organization anticipates and plans for its future. The result is a written document that guides the association toward its future goals. This chapter opens with an overview of the strategic planning process, then takes a look at what strategic planning is, what an association can reasonably expect from the process, and what it is not.

Overview of strategic planning

The initial recommendation to undertake strategic planning in a trade or professional association may come from the governing body, from the appointed administrator or administrative staff, or from interests expressed by the membership. Or, it may come from a determination on the part of the group's membership and leadership to harness the industry's or the profession's strengths and take charge of its future.

Whatever the underlying reason, strategic planning

needs to be embraced by the group's leadership and publicized and "sold" to the members as well as to the employees. This early stage involves action by the group's officers, communication with employees, face-to-face discussions with future participants in the process and dissemination of information to the general membership. As it becomes clear that a decision to undertake strategic planning is imminent, the association's professional staff must prepare to administer it. One individual should be responsible for formalizing the planning process, identifying and inviting participants, scheduling meetings and establishing deadlines, and ensuring that necessary follow-up steps are taken. This person may be the senior administrator or his or her designee, or some associations employ a consultant from a local business or from amongst the organization's membership. Some organizations have utilized an outside consultant, in which case a member should be assigned to act as liaison with the consultant.

Strategic planning has various time considerations ranging from the long-term to the short-term. In the early stages of the planning process, participants look ahead and predict what may happen in their respective fields over the long-term, the next three to five years. Later, they will have to establish short-term strategies for moving in the direction the membership wants to go over the next year.

A formal strategic planning process has the following results, each of which will be examined in future chapters:

1. a mission statement for the organization
2. an environmental scan and conclusions about future scenarios in a three- to five-year period
3. basic goals for the time period in the scan, and goals for the coming one-year period

4. strategies and actions that will move the organization toward the goals

5. implementation plans that assign responsibilities for actions

These results are usually formalized in the written strategic plan; examples are found throughout this book and in its appendices. The process of formalizing a mission statement, forecasting scenarios, and setting goals for the organization will involve numerous meetings and other forums for the exchange of ideas. Participants in these forums should be representatives of all aspects of the association: officers and members, staff, and others as appropriate. Deciding on action steps and detailing implementation plans are usually the responsibility of the professional management.

The written plan generally goes through several drafts, with the final plan approved by the Board of Directors. Once approved and published, the plan becomes a blueprint for action and decision making as the association moves toward its desired future.

What strategic planning is

As noted earlier, formal strategic planning in an organization must be regarded as a product and a process. As a process, planning is a means of prompting thought, provoking internal examination, and facilitating decision making. In an association setting, the process may include the identification of key persons who should be involved, or from whom input should he sought. This typically would include, in addition to those regularly involved in the operations of the association, others who have valuable information, key perceptions, and/or large bases of support.

Assembling such a diverse and potentially adversarial

group may initially delay the process rather than facilitate it. However, it is better to invite and resolve conflict early in the discussion and decision making stages than to confront it while trying to implement the resulting programs. In fact, diversity of perspective in the planning process frequently offers significant benefits. A plan that is the result of debate and negotiation often represents a compromise in which opposing points of view have embraced an acceptable alternative.

The plan itself then becomes not only a compendium of program directions, philosophies, and strategies, but also a symbol of unity. The plan represents a collectively supported vision of the organization's future and the most acceptable formula for allocating the always-scarce resources. This is particularly true as an association begins to conduct formal strategic planning sessions for the first time.

For groups that have used the process before, strategic planning becomes a style of organizational operation, a guide for decision making, a "systematic means of coping with uncertainty," [1] and a determinant of project feasibility and success. Finally, it can be a structure for long-term growth within which more immediate directions are highlighted. Thus, a three-year plan may describe the overall direction for an organization for the ensuing three-year period as well as determine the structure of the more imminent, one-year phase of the program.

A plan is a vision – a vision of the future and of what the membership and its governing and management bodies can accomplish within the confines of future realities, as observed from the present.

What strategic planning is not

First and foremost, neither the process nor the product of strategic planning is a mechanism that relieves decision makers of their ongoing responsibilities. Strategic planning defines the most likely conditions within which decisions must be made, and it can highlight the potential effects of various decisions. But it cannot prescribe specific courses of action. Given the best information, the best analysis and comprehension, and even the best luck, the plan can only refine our understanding of options. Final decisions will be made by individuals and groups who, even with the best information, remain human and must make difficult choices from opposing options. There is no guarantee that they will make the right selections. There is also no guarantee that the data will remain constant or that conditions won't change. There is no guarantee that the program designed to fit a projected scenario of the future will succeed. On the other hand, an organization that relies solely on intuitive decision making can succeed. Although more informed decisions are possible through planning, and although the planning process enhances the chance of making the best decisions, it does not ensure success. But it does improve the chances.

Planning is not a panacea for resolving organizational conflicts. Although it may draw opposing factions closer through negotiation, it will not unite them, nor will it create consensus on philosophy or programming.

In situations in which resources are scarce, strategic planning will not increase them. It may be useful as a means of stretching resources, both human and capital. It can be an effective tool in reaching conclusions about which resources can have the most immediate impact when spent on problems or to take advantage of opportunities, but it cannot expand finite resources. However, the planning process may help to identify additional resources – state, federal, private, volunteer – and to maximize existing resources.

As a process, strategic planning is not a one-time endeavor. It must be constant and ongoing. As the environment changes, or as our understanding of the environment becomes more clear, the plan can be amended and its resulting actions adjusted. The process must continue because the environment is always in flux. To plan once is to be unprepared. What was once inflexibility becomes rigidity. To maintain flexibility, an association must constantly analyze the past, scrutinize the present, and prepare for the future.

One-time plans intended to serve as long-term guides in the 1980s might have failed to anticipate many of the changes that have occurred since then that directly impact the membership of various associations in various ways, some positive, others less so. Not many planners foresaw the changes in the international political situation that have occurred, or the manner and rapidity of technological change, or the extent to which national political changes have affected various decisions about budgets, programs, and general visions of the future.

In brief, planning must be regarded only as a means of facilitating decision making and clarifying options. It cannot change the conditions of the environment nor eliminate uncertainty. But it can create understanding, promote compromise, provide flexibility, and formulate a vision of the future and the best means of achieving it.

Pitfalls to avoid in strategic planning

As in any major organizational initiative, there are pitfalls in strategic planning. Awareness of some common faults in the process and product of strategic planning can help planners avoid some of them.

Regarding the plan as an end point The first pitfall to avoid in strategic planning, which frequently occurs in organizations new to the planning process, is the inclination to regard the written plan as the end of the process. The plan —the product itself— is simply the structure resulting from examining potential opportunities and threats in the future environment. The greatest benefits of planning derive from the process: the discussions, analyses, and thought processes leading to decisions. Too often, plans are written, shelved, and forgotten. They must be disseminated to those affected, explained, and promoted if they are to be embraced and supported by those who will be expected to implement them and those who will be affected by them.

Regarding the plan as unalterable A second pitfall to avoid is regarding the plan as unalterable. Plans and their analyses need to be reviewed constantly, and performance against planned goals and objectives requires ongoing and rigorous scrutiny. If conditions change, or if actual performance varies too much from the stated goals and objectives, local leaders need to assess why this is happening, and then decide how to react, and what new programs to implement, targets to set, or resources to redistribute. To continue to pursue programs that are not proceeding as expected or objectives that are not being met only invites further divergence from plan to actual. As H. L. Mencken once admonished, "For every problem, there is a solution that is simple, neat, and wrong." [2] Continuous diligence can yield the right solutions at the right time.

Failing to question assumptions Another frequent error is to permit preconceptions or other pre-established perspectives to be incorporated into plans without being thoroughly questioned. This often occurs when the source of that perspective is regarded as venerable or unimpeachable or is too highly placed in the organization to be questioned. Not challenging underlying assumptions, however, produces a plan which is no more than a written justification for presumption. Within the association context, for example, the ranking individual may be the senior administrator or an elected member. Such individuals often have superior ability to see the "big picture" but, because of the level of their responsibilities, may not see the details, while others who work on specific issues and programs, at lower organizational levels, probably do. Regrettably, their views are not always sought or, if they are, they may be disregarded because they are counter to assumptions held by persons at higher levels of the organization. Avoiding this pitfall of failing to question assumptions requires a conscious decision to solicit input from all levels and to accord all intelligence full consideration.

Failing to gain organizational commitment Another pitfall, especially for organizations beginning strategic planning for the first time, is the lack of a full conceptual commitment to the process at all levels of the organization. As suggested earlier, it is vital that input be obtained from front line staff because of their perspectives and because it is they who will ultimately implement the programs prescribed by the plan and strive to achieve its goals and objectives. Middle managers must also provide input. One observer has noted: "The majority of managers in individual business units see little relation between what they do (and why they do it) and the corporate objectives and goals. This situation is what is best known as the 'planning gap.'"[3] Involving individuals throughout the organization helps ensure their commitment. The most senior officials must also "buy in" to the process and communicate full support for the product. This sense of their commitment to the plan, and to planning in general, permeates all levels of the organization and generates further support for the goals and directions. Anything less than full support for the plan by the elected and senior appointed officials will be detected by program staff and constituents and will dilute the effectiveness of the programs. Anything less than enthusiasm for the process will be felt in subsequent planning cycles.

Adopting the wrong goals Still another pitfall is the adoption of strategies which, while good ideas, might damage the organization's effectiveness. Strategic planners must be cautious in recommending only strategies which warrant taking the accompanying risks and which have the potential to be implemented. Association planners will do well to heed Jan Carlzon, president of Scandinavian Air Service, who wrote that the hardest thing to do in strategic planning is to abandon a good idea that doesn't fit the time or place.[4]

When a representative organization embarks on a course of action for which it has insufficient funding, knowledge, experience, or political support, it loses its capacity for quality performance not only in the new program, but also in existing programs. Overextending can cause disastrous misallocations of resources and embarrassing conflicts. Many a business has become too diversified, and the same can happen to an association that attempts to resolve all of its members' needs too quickly. The wiser approach to planning is to do a few things well and to move forward in small measures. For an association, membership services often provide the first tier of responsibility. As resources become available to provide more than these essential levels of service, other good ideas can be investigated and implemented.

Associations and their planners might keep in mind the lament of Charles de Gaulle: "How can anyone rule a country that produces 266 varieties of cheese?"[5] Given the diversity of member services and demands, planners must be alert for inconsistencies among individual elements of a plan. The various components of a total plan "are not always directly related to one another and can even work at cross purposes."[6] All of these potential pitfalls apply both to trade and professional associations and to private businesses.

Imposing unnecessary limitations There is another pitfall which may occur more often in association management. It is not unusual for such organizations to become confined in their thinking because of various limits on them. The breadth of local operations is often well defined in law, ordinance, regulation, or the originating charter. A business, given adequate capacity, resources, and motivation, can try new markets or product lines. It can sell unprofitable divisions, close some plants, or shut down operations entirely. Such alternatives are not always feasible for associations. Another limitation is the lack of funding, which impedes change even when decision makers are motivated and prepared to implement new strategies. This lack of resources may to lead to viewing the appropriate future course of action as "business as usual." This attitude may be appropriate if it refers to the scope of operations, but it should not be the approach to seeking means of providing services. Associations can strive to approach old problems with new solutions and to perform ongoing tasks in innovative and more efficient ways. These initiatives will be the result of strategic planning.

1. Jan Carlzon, Moments of Truth (New York: Ballinger Publishing Company, 1987)
2. The Oxford Dictionary of Quotations, 3rd ed. (Oxford: Oxford University Press, 1980), p. 173
3. Cass Bettinger, "Use Corporate Culture to Trigger High Performance," *Journal of Business Strategy* 10, no. 2 (March/April 1989) 38-42.
4. Carlzon, Moments of Truth, p.55.
5. Oxford Dictionary of Quotations, p. 173.
6. Peter M. Scott and Walter W. Simpson "Connecting Overall Corporate Planning to Individual Business Units," *Public Utilities Fortnightly* 123, no. 12 (June 8, 1987): 27.

Chapter 2

The Strategic Plan: Analysis

In discussing the elements of a strategic plan, a note of caution is important. The reader of this text should be aware that the concepts involved have varying labels. For example, where one plan uses the term *goals, objectives,* and *strategies,* another might express the same concepts as the *vision, targets,* and *action steps.* Where this book uses the term *environmental scan,* a strategic plan for one association used the term *alternative approaches* for viewing future environments. What is referred to in this text as *goals, objectives,* and *strategies* was referred to in that association's plan as *recommended solutions.* Funding consideration in that plan corresponded to *implementation plan* in this text. *Stakeholders* can be called *role players. Environmental scans* can be called *needs assessments* or *SWOT analyses* (SWOT is an acronym for Strengths, Weaknesses, Opportunities, and Threats). There is no consistent usage in either the professional or the academic literature. To become preoccupied with the terminology is to be distracted from the actual meaning. The reader should consider concepts, however they are labeled.

Associations and their stakeholders

"Stakeholder" is a term that has evolved in the literature on strategic planning and in other fields. It refers to persons who have a direct interest in what is done by an organization.

For a business, the stakeholders are typically the owners, the managers and employees, the vendors and distributors, and the customers. For an association, the list will include the following at the very least:

1. Elected Board members and officers of the association
    a. Chairman of the Board
    b. Executive Committee members
    c. Committee chairs
    d. Representatives of affiliated associations
2. Other officials
    a. Senior professional management staff
    b. Other association officials, related or unrelated
    c. Federal, state, or local officials with oversight responsibilities
    d. Other officials as appropriate
3. Others
    a. Member representatives other than Board members
    b. Those in the field or with related interests but who are not members
    c. Consumers or other groups which procure goods or services from the membership
    d. Others as appropriate

Businesses must constantly decide where or how to expand, contract, seek new opportunity, or change operations; so must associations. As they do so, planners in both must receive input from, and consider the effects on, their stakeholders.

A difference for the association, of course, is that the decisions will ultimately be reached at the elected levels in the organization. This means directors, councils and boards. Unlike the business strategic planner, whose sole or primary consideration is which combinations of goods and services will generate the maximum financial return, the association planner must be aware of different dynamics. Decision makers in associations generally feel obligated to various constituencies among the stakeholders. They may be driven by values of service or dedication to a field or cause unlike the values that drive business decisions. Thus, some decisions will require resources for political or even emotional reasons. Some may fly in the face of logic based entirely on financial reasoning.

It is important for strategic planners to be cognizant of the dynamics of such decision making. It may even behoove those responsible for the plan to hold early, informal discussions with key decision makers in order to identify such possibilities and determine whether to address them in the plan. In any event, planning and program implementation cannot always reflect simple cost-benefit analyses alone. Since the plans and programs will reflect some political and emotional factors, the architects of the plan must be prepared and instructed in these matters.

Those who manage the strategic planning process for the association should solicit and coordinate input from stakeholders efficiently and systematically, identify various levels of involvement for all of the potential participants, keep all interested parties informed of progress, solicit and incorporate feedback, develop and gauge support and opposition, and propose and encourage compromise.

In the environmental scan, it is important to be aware of the plans of others. This is especially true for an association that is active in legislative affairs or that represents an industry or profession that is undergoing dramatic technological, or other, change.

Stakeholder involvement in the larger, more diverse associations requires similar but broader representation in the planning process. For example, a few business representatives might well represent the perspective of an entire business community. Rather than representing their specific businesses, they might be agents of the local Chamber of Commerce, for example. Other umbrella organizations might also represent a larger constituency of members, regulatory officials, customers, or other stakeholders.

Stakeholders in an internal strategic plan

An exception to the inclusive approach may occur when strategic planning is designed with the specific intent of taking an inward look at an association and its services. Often, such planning is expedient as a first step to set the agenda for future, broader planning efforts. In such cases, it is often the senior staff, officers, and major committees that take part in the process. The following section shows the structure and roles of the groups participating in the strategic planning of one association, the Chicago-based Academy of General Dentistry:

1. Generally, the Council on Long Ranging Planning meets once a year, alternating the primary focus of the meeting. At one meeting, it will identify trends affecting the profession, and at the next it will identify member needs by analyzing the results of the bi-annual

Membership Survey. At every meeting, it reviews and recommends revisions to the entire Long Range Plan, and refers issues to other Academy agencies.

2. Each council and committee takes responsibility for identifying trends impacting issues under its purview, and for reviewing the Long Range Plan every time it meets. The council or committee should take into account any trends it identifies, any trends referred from the Council on Long Range Planning, the activities under its jurisdiction, and recommendations from staff, to revise the specific objectives and strategies for the goals under its purview.

3. Periodically, the Executive Committee identifies trends impacting the dental profession.

4. The Board of Trustees evaluates the recommendations made by councils and committees and approves revisions to the Long Range Plan. The Board also approves referrals from the Council on Long Range Planning to other Academy agencies. Periodically, this body also identifies trends impacting the profession.

5. The Budget and Finance Committee sets fiscal priorities for the Academy programs each year, which determines which strategies will be funded.

6. The House of Delegates adopts the Academy programs and budget each year.

7. Staff objectives are developed on the basis of the actions of the House of Delegates and the Long Range Plan.

The text of strategic plans often states explicitly that the process needs to belong to all of the stakeholders in an organization rather than simply to the staff or elected leadership. The latter is sometimes perceived as being controlling, short-term in its thinking, too closely tied to budgets, or even in an ivory tower and out-of-touch. The preferred approach to strategic planning is consensus from the membership, the staff, and the elected board and officers.

Is it important to have a broad range of input into an organization's strategic planning process? It may be. Strategic planners must decide who to involve, how to involve them, and how to solicit input from those who are not directly involved. It will and ought to be different everywhere. One association, the Houston-based International Facility Management Association, described their "customer and stakeholder segmentation" in the executive summary of the IFMA strategic plan:

> The environment continuously redefines the nature of the workplace. This includes the solutions, techniques, and even the required expertise necessary to deal with new challenges. IFMA must respond creatively by realigning itself in terms of issues, roles, and competencies. One major challenge facing IFMA is the wide spectrum of people, industries, disciplines and interests represented by the current membership. Add to this mix evolving technologies, fierce global competitiveness and the changing nature of jobs and work. Without a clear focus on a few critical issues that will supply superior value to its membership, there is no guarantee for IFMA's survival, let alone success.
>
> Customers:
>
> 1. Less experienced professionals whose desire is to learn new skills and broaden competencies that are generic in nature. This builds their knowledge base

and enhances their professional advancement.

2. Senior professionals whose interest is networking with peers and learning about specific, in-depth topics. They usually have significant experience and possess substantial knowledge. IFMA membership keeps them current in the field.

3. Individuals and companies who support the facility management profession with value-added products, services, research, and training that result in mutually beneficial business relationships.

4. Educators who possess and develop facility management knowledge and expertise and share their knowledge with students and practitioners. In addition, students who seek this information to become the facility managers of the future.

Stakeholders:

1. The business entity and its leadership who are responsible for the client's organizational and business results

2. The governmental regulatory agencies, public utilities, and related associations

3. The professional staff that manage IFMA as a non-profit association

The growing importance of stakeholder input into the process is evident. Increased member communication with their representative trade or professional association can be measured to demonstrate the growing interest of member stakeholders in the planning and management of their own associations.

In addition to determining how to ensure the optimum input for everyone and for every group, those who organize the planning process must also consider the most efficient size and composition of the planning group and the type of group process to employ for gathering information. This will be discussed in Chapter 5, "Organizational Considerations."

The inherent beliefs of an organization

The inherent beliefs and values of the most influential members of an organization help structure planning and other activities. They are what Michael Kami refers to as "psychographics and aspirations."[1] These beliefs are so ingrained in individuals as to be unidentifiable to them personally or to their colleagues. However, the awareness of such beliefs by those involved in strategic planning is critical. Planners must recognize the importance of these beliefs and attempt to identify and comprehend them. Often this means knowing the point of view of top officials who may not even be involved in the planning deliberations.

Much research has been devoted to identifying the inherent beliefs of organizations. Of course, they are not easy to define. The seminal study is *In Search of Excellence*, in which Peters and Waterman highlight seven "values" usually found in "excellent" companies:

- a belief in being the best
- a belief in the importance of attention to detail
- a belief in the importance of the individual
- a belief in superior quality and service
- a belief in innovation and the willingness to support failure
- a belief in the importance of informality to enhance communication
- a belief in the importance of economic growth and profit.[2]

The fourth of these points — an orientation to service — tends to be more prevalent in associations than in business. Consider the following array of values, or "principles of action," as listed in the strategic plan of the

International Society of Optical Engineering, located in Bellingham, Washington:

Continuous Improvement:
- search continually for ways to improve quality and value to the customer
- improve processes as well as results
- strive for excellence
- constantly upgrade staff skills and capabilities

Member/Customer Oriented:
- meet all requirements
- exceed expectation where possible
- provide maximum value to members as a top priority

Inclusive:
- serve the broad technical and economic global communities

Ethical:
- conduct all business in an ethical manner

Innovative:
- be creative and clever; value the new and different
- accomplish all things in a superior way
- take calculated risks

Flexible:
- do what works
- be adaptable and open to change

Responsive:
- meet all schedule commitments
- do what the customer asks; meet their needs
- be decisive; take action quickly

Mutuality of Benefit:
- parties must benefit fairly and proportionately from decisions, actions, and agreements

Collaborative:
- seek and value new associations
- focus on the common objective

Fiscally Responsible:
- assure the financial health of the Society
- provide the resources needed to accomplish the Society's goals and objectives

One association's basic premises may reflect concern for the diversity of the program offerings, high standards of quality in service or representation, close coordination with the public and private sectors, and maintaining the richness of the relevant traditions, values, and history. Another may recognize the need to grow while preserving the quality of professional services to their constituency. Such values as friendliness, responsiveness, and seriousness of purpose reflect a need for strategies intended to change some operational elements while preserving others.

The elements of the underlying beliefs of an organization have been summarized in various ways. One such classification includes:

- attitudes toward change
- degree of consensus between senior officials
- standards and values
- concern for people
- attitudes toward openness and communication
- conflict resolution style (i.e., win-lose versus win-win)
- group orientation toward the market, the consumer
- excitement, pride, "esprit de corps"
- commitment
- teamwork[3]

In an association, the guiding principles of the organization will regularly manifest themselves in the selection of new programs and in the decision to continue existing programs. They will, therefore, ultimately affect the members' feelings about the association and its relative value. Both the senior policymakers and those beneath them who implement the programs hold inherent beliefs that are reflected collectively in the quality of their services. Individuals may vary in their attitudes toward change, spirit of cooperation, respect for all members of the association, and styles of leadership. If the individuals' beliefs are consistent with the philosophy and intent of the plan, the operations stand a better chance of achieving success.

Planners need to understand the degree to which a general philosophical consensus exists among key elected and appointed officials of the organization. If change is necessary, should it be incremental or massive? Is there an acceptance of program expansion, fiscal conservatism, a greater presence in legislative deliberations? As association planners consider new strategies, they must understand the collective will to accept change, whether slow or dramatic. This understanding can help them clarify goals and objectives before allocating resources.

Collective values, standards of behavior, and perceptions of human needs affect the manner in which programs are selected and targets identified. The strategic planner or planning committee should be aware of the operating styles of the association's leaders and their attitudes toward seeking compromise, open and regular communication, and the level of commitment to the general advancement of the association's aims.

Understanding these factors will not dictate the direction an association will set or which programs will be selected. It will, however, illuminate the context within which those decisions will be made. It may help to identify where compromises may be feasible. In the current vernacular, in order to know where you're going, it is vital to understand "where you're coming from." Appendix I includes, for purposes of reference, the listed inherent beliefs from the plans of two organizations: the Reston-based Music Educators National Conference and the Door and Hardware Institute, located in Chantilly, Virginia.

The Mission Statement

The mission statement of an organization reflects its essential purpose – its "raison d'etre." For this reason, it should seldom change. Mission statements, though not always labeled as such, can be found in any number of documents. They may be referred to as the organizations corporate vision, its purpose, or its objective.

In the private sector, statements for businesses may be found in originating charters, annual reports, or stockholder communications. Such essential descriptions of a company's purpose tend to focus on profits, commercial leadership, return on investment, market share, and quality service.

For the association, the mission statement can be found in the organization's charter or tax code documentation. Sometimes, they may be found in annual budgets, policy documents, and long-term planning records. Many such statements have a common theme: to provide the maximum quality and quantity of member services for the lowest dues possible. Others may address various charitable or educational goals.

Some examples are usually as instructive as a definition. Witness the following examples of mission statements that have been taken from several associations' plans:

International Facilities Management Association:

> IFMA promotes and encourages excellence in workplace management procedures and in the people, place, and process to advance organizational goals.

Music Educators National Conference:

> To advance music education by encouraging the study and making of music by all Americans.

American Pharmaceutical Association:

> To serve its members, to enhance pharmacists' ability to provide pharmaceutical care, and to further

the public's recognition of the profession's value.

American Machine Tool Distributors' Association:

To provide marketers of manufacturing technology the essential services necessary to develop and perpetuate distribution businesses that make vital contributions to North American manufacturing.

Academy of General Dentistry:

To serve the needs and represent the interests of general dentists and to foster their continued proficiency through quality continuing dental education in order to better serve the public.

Such statements should be concise but encompassing enough to withstand the changes wrought by time and shifts in critical environmental factors. The importance of being concise and specific in the mission statement can not be overemphasized. Tuegoe and Tobia have addressed this need. If you were a manager who had to make decisions about product, market positioning and allocating resources, they ask, what guidance would you get from this plank in the strategy of one major US company? "Our business is the creation of machine and methods to help find solutions to the increasingly complex problems of business, government, science, space exploration, education, medicine, and nearly every other area of human endeavor."[4]

The ability to be quickly scanned and understood is important in a mission statement. Equally vital is that a mission statement be enduring. As will be discussed in a later chapter, an organization's goals and objectives must be sensitive to environmental factors to permit flexibility and response to changing threats and opportunities. This all takes place, however, within the context of a constant mission. Businesses still seek maximum profits and returns on investments. Associations will wish to provide the highest quality services possible for the lowest possible dues.

Text continues on page 38

Environmental scanning

The Information needed for conducting an environmental scan can be taken from a number of reliable sources. For strategic planners in the association community, one obvious and dependable source for data and insights is the American Society of Association Executives. The material below is extracted from one ASAE publication and characterizes one of numerous trends discussed in the book.

TREND 6.1: Proliferation of Single-Issue Politics Continues

Single-issue politics drives much of the legislative agenda at the state and national levels by forcing the hands of legislators. With sufficient strength, the advocates or enemies of an interest can demand and get action. This happens when an issue has reached public prominence. For example, the issue of gun control versus the right to keep and bear arms, and the pro-choice versus the pro-life movements, have advocacy groups largely or entirely devoted to promoting a single point of view...Often grassroots advocacy takes off, magnifying and propelling an issue.

Usually, organizations push a single agenda without compromise, even though compromise is the key to progress in the U.S. political system. Associations often support single-issue politics, which may make them less effective over the long term. Associations will have to learn to work in coalitions, expand their issues agendas, and acknowledge varying stances on issues to be effective in the long term.

The government's agenda follows the development of public issues. Every issue that gains prominence arises, finds a niche, develops to a full-blown issue, and then gets crowded out by the arrival of new issues. In that sense, every issue fits into an ecology of other issues.

Because new issues may drive out old issues, pushing a single issue may be an all-or-nothing effort, inherently risky. The public will eventually grow tired of the issue and lose interest, thus putting a premium on building multigroup coalitions to support critical association agendas and keep important issues in front of the public and legislators.

Issues arise as latent concerns. An issue really takes

off when someone or some group frames the issue and puts it in a form recognizable by the public, often giving it a catchy name like Right-to-Life or Pro-Choice. Word then spreads as the issue is communicated. It finds a niche in the public mindset and on the airwaves. It then becomes a full-blown public issue. Eventually, new issues will come along and crowd out this issue, which has not been resolved.

Potential Countertrends

Movements supporting sweeping change, the reinvention of government, or new or renewed political groups with comprehensive agendas could offset the effects of single-issue politics. They could thereby dislodge an issue central to the mission of a particular association.

Implications for Associations of the Proliferation of Single-Issue Politics

- Associations may find their membership becoming more politicized on particular issues, which will be divisive. This problem requires the close attention of association leaders. Leaders will often have to decide on the winners and losers among issues in reaching policy decisions
- Coalitions are a better alternative to today's political action committees (PACs). The need to build coalitions among interest groups will be greater because the greater number of groups and their diverging agendas may make it difficult for any one group to prevail
- Associations may want to set up their own PACs, as many have already done, to promote their own public policy agendas
- PACs may need to innovate in information delivery, especially if their lobbying and political contributions are restricted
- Associations will need to learn how to identify latent concerns that may become issues. They must then watch as the issues become public. Associations should learn how to push pertinent issues up the development scale
- Should associations cultivate single-issue groups within the membership? Can they be brought under the umbrella?

Changes in mission statements may occur when a major event takes place. For a business, this may occur when a company enters a new market or when a whole industry is deregulated. For an association, major changes occur infrequently. One such change, however, might be the successful accomplishment of the initial mission, the defeat of a targeted disease, or the introduction of new technologies to a field. In the case of such a significant change, the mission statement may require amendment.

The mission statement communicates the organizations purpose to a variety of audiences and forms the basis for the goals, objectives, and implementation plans. The existence of a clearly communicated mission can allow employees and other stakeholders to stretch to reach new heights without losing sight of the principles on which the association was founded or has historically operated.

Environmental Scanning

Any organization exists and operates in environments that affect its ability to be successful. Organizations try to picture the future environmental context within which goals and objectives will be set and strategies implemented. They must anticipate as nearly as possible what will occur in the future and construct their plan in a manner consistent with the most likely scenarios.

Their planning will be complicated by the fact that environmental factors undergo constant change. Unemployment rises and falls, demographics shift, and federal, state, and local legislation may become impactful without much notice. Not only do these factors change, but they may do so in unpredictable ways. Furthermore, the future may be affected by them. Such an example for business was the collapse of the Soviet Union and the subsequent reduction in federal defense procurement.

Strategic planning enables an organization to cope better with such fluctuations — both those which are anticipated and those which are not — and to take maximum advantage of such changes.

An organization's environment has several concurrent contexts. There is the organizational context, the factors which exist within the organization itself. External contexts include the industry (in this case, the general practice of association management) and geographic contexts (local, state, region, nation, and/or global). Because of these multiple contexts, the impact of environmental change frequently tends to be more exponential than arithmetic. For this reason, planners sometimes use computer programs to assist in scanning to discuss and review their future needs.

The process of environmental scanning is the same for a public agency as for an association as for a profit-making business. Whereas a business will scan the environment for factors affecting its ability to make a profit, an association will be concerned with membership services and changes requiring new patterns of resource allocation.

The breadth of environmental factors to scan in each association will be extensive and, of course, the content will vary considerably. The table of contents from the Arlington, Virginia-based American Association of School Administrators' scan is illustrated in Appendix II. It is extracted from a volume published by AASA to guide its members in their specific strategic planning processes. It clearly demonstrates the factors of relevance for its members, however one might imagine how many of those factors would not bear relevance to the planning process of other associations.

The scanning matrix There are numerous models to follow in reviewing the several environments within which planning and program operations will occur. These are merely tools to facilitate the scanning process; they may or may not actually appear in the final written document. One type of scanning matrix cited in business-oriented strategic planning literature is illustrated in Figure 2.1 It is applicable for association planning as well.

At the top of the matrix in Figure 2.1, identified by letters, are the various environments in which an association may operate and plan:

A. Internal (the specific association)

B. Association management generally

C. Local (the community)

D. Regional

E. State

F. National

G. Global

Following is a list of environmental factors to be considered in creating an association's strategic plan:

1. Economic and financial
2. Demographic
3. Technological
4. Legal and regulatory
5. Social and cultural
6. Competitive
7. Managerial
8. Other

The matrix can be used to list factors that are important in each environment. For reference, each "cell" in the matrix is labeled with the appropriate letter and number.

The matrix illustrated in Figure 2.1 is designed to be very general. Associations may have several environments to scan under the various headings. Some factors will be unique to some groups; for example, large international organizations may not need to be tuned in to local factors beyond merely paying taxes and such mundane matters. Conversely, local groups may need to spend very little time giving consideration to factors in the national and global environments. All relevant environments should be represented by stakeholders who participate in the planning process. The matrix will provide direction for those planners conducting the scans of the various environments. The review and assessment of each scan can then take place within the context of the other areas noted in the matrix. Structuring the scanning process in this way permits an orderly review.

It is often helpful to conduct the scan as a two-step process. The first step is to consider each cell in the matrix and list the relevant points to be considered. The second is to extract the opportunities and threats in summary fashion. Some cells may not be relevant to future goals and objectives, or the relevant information already appears in another cell. This does not matter. It is simply important that all pertinent information receive full consideration. Because some associations may have a broad range of functions and responsibilities, the matrix can become large and cluttered as all conceivable factors are listed. Some of the items associations will need to consider in the environmental scan are listed in Figure 2.2. The list is intended to suggest the type of intelligence that is relevant to strategic planning; it is not intended to be all-inclusive or to suggest that all this information must be compiled.

Association strategic planners must carefully consider the factors to be analyzed. The environmental scan is the basis for better understanding the future. With it, planners can determine the best goals, objectives, and strategies possible with given resources.

To show how the process works, later chapters will build on the example shown in Figure 2.2. The environmental factors listed here will be used as the basis for sample goals, objectives, strategies, and implementation plans.

The internal scan

An environmental scan is frequently divided into an external scan, in which strategic planners view the world "out there," and an internal scan, in which they examine the strengths and weaknesses of the organization itself. The external scan is often easier; many organizations are adept at studying facts. The internal scan, however, involves intangible political and emotional factors in addition to financial and demographic considerations.

One important component of an internal scan is the members' perception of the value of the services being

	Environments			
	Internal	Association	Local	Regional
Factors	A	B	C	D
Economic and Financial	A-1	B-1	C-1	D-1
Demographic	A-2	B-2	C-2	D-2
Technological	A-3	B-3	C-3	D-3
Legal and Regulatory	A-4	B-4	C-4	D-4
Social and Cultural	A-5	B-5	C-5	D-5
Competitive	A-6	B-6	C-6	D-6
Managerial	A-7	B-7	C-7	D-7
Other	A-8	B-8	C-8	D-8

Figure 2.1 Environmental scanning matrix

provided. An association's leadership can go a long way in the accurate assessment of members' attitudes by conducting interviews and surveys. These need not be elaborate or expensive although, as membership grows and/or issues become broader and more complex, such surveys do tend to be more formal and detailed.

A member attitude survey can reveal valuable information about preferences, concerns, and general direction. Two or more surveys, completed at regular intervals, can demonstrate patterns in choices and shifts in attitudes.

The Brick Institute of America in Reston conducted a mail survey of its membership prior to initiating its strategic planning discussions. A second survey of its regional office staff was also conducted, with the results being quite similar. The findings demonstrated a number of common themes:

Text continued on page 52

	Environments		
	State	National	Global
Factors	E	F	G
Economic and Financial	E-1	F-1	G-1
Demographic	E-2	F-2	G-2
Technological	E-3	F-3	G-3
Legal and Regulatory	E-4	F-4	G-4
Social and Cultural	E-5	F-5	G-5
Competitive	E-6	F-6	G-6
Managerial	E-7	F-7	G-7
Other	E-8	F-8	G-8

Figure 2.1 continued

Internal environment

Economic and financial factors (A-1)

1. trends in member dues revenues
2. trends in revenues generated by programs
3. trends in advertising support for the association's publications
4. status of grant and foundation support
5. trends in expenditure levels and service demands
6. trends in employees' salaries and fringe benefits
7. trends in the costs of the organization's insurance and other premiums
8. performance of investment portfolio
9. debt service requirements
10. expenses associated with office space and the relative costs of alternatives

Demographic factors (A-2)

1. number of employees by classification, skill level, and tenure
2. composition of association workforce by grade, cross-tabulated by age, race, and sex
3. number of employees eligible or near-eligible for retirement

Technological factors (A-3)

1. state of computer and other technology in the association
2. areas where resources could be saved through technological advances, and the costs associated with doing so
3. areas where technology will be replaced or upgraded
4. skills likely to be in demand by the association in the future, and the gap between the present and future

Legal and regulatory factors (A-4)

1. federal and state regulations or laws which will affect the demand for change or new or increased levels of effort
2. legislation or regulations at any level that will facilitate progress, permit taking advantage of opportunities, or avoid threats to the success of the plan

Figure 2.2. Environmental factors to consider in strategic planning.

3. federal and state legislators and officials with influence in law-making, and whether they are accessible and supportive
4. positions or individuals in the local political arena requiring attention, support, or opposition

Social and cultural factors (A-5)

1. extent to which staff and programs reflect the social and cultural composition of the membership and the local community
2. staff morale

Competitive factors (A-6)

1. programs in place for succession and promotion

Managerial factors (A-7)

1. strengths and weaknesses of management staff
2. alignment of current managerial talent and structure with future programs and needs
3. areas in which management training could be beneficial
4. specific areas of interest to this year's chairman
5. old and new services in demand (or not) by the members

Association management environment

Economic and financial factors (B4)

1. trends in membership and dues payments
2. general trends in federal funding for health research

Demographic factors (B-2)

1. availability of recent graduates with degrees in association management, communications, or other relevant fields

Technological factors (B-3)

1. new computer or other technological applications for association functions
2. technological applications of other associations that could be useful and replicable

Figure 2.2. Continued

Legal and regulatory factors (B-4)

1. issues being followed by the American Society of Association Executives (ASAE), state or local organizations, or others
2. legal issues and decisions in other organizations with potential precedential implications
3. trends in other associations toward the collection of user fees for selected services, meetings, and publications
4. changes in the IRS code and other relevant tax codes

Social and cultural factors (B-5)

1. growth or decline of general interest in the social, cultural, medical, and other positions being addressed by various associations

Competitive factors (B-6)

1. trends in association memberships, generally, as well as dues payments
2. federal, state, local, or private funding available on a competitive basis

Managerial factors (B-7)

1. management issues identified by professionals in the field of association management and the specific professional and technical areas of association management
2. management issues being followed by professional organizations in the field (e.g., ASAE)

Local environment

Economic and financial factors (C-1)

1. key local economic indicators, including employment, job growth, and consumer confidence as they affect the association and its membership
2. positions of local Chambers of Commerce and other business organizations on issues relevant to the association
2. the costs of doing business in the present location, relative to the value of the location

Figure 2.2. Continued

Demographic factors C-2)

1. availability of required work force skills levels at acceptable wage rates

Technological Factors (C-3)

1. for associations with a technology business constituency, is the business community in the headquarters location compatible?

Legal and regulatory factors (C-4)

1. changes in local tax codes affecting the association and its membership
2. proposed legislative or regulatory issues of concern to those in the association members' fields of interest

Social and cultural factors (C-5)

1. community acceptance of the specific aims of the association

Competitive factors (C-6)

1. other local representative groups competing for membership

Managerial factors (C-7)

1. availability of training and retraining opportunities
2. presence and effectiveness of a local society of association executives, chamber of commerce, or other business coordinating group

Other factors (C-8)

1. local infrastructure, sites, etc. that relate to the specific aims of the association
2. the availability of air service and other transportation networks that will enable members to attend committee meetings and that will facilitate staff travel to members' sites
3. the quality and quantity of hotel and conference space and the necessary amenities locally to support the association's meeting needs

Figure 2.2. Continued

Regional Environment

Economic and social factors (D-1)

1. costs for the use of meeting facilities and amenities in the region to the association and its members
2. regional business patterns that will affect the association and the businesses of the members

Demographic factors (D-2)

1. migration in and out of the region of persons in relevant trades or professions (i.e., prospective members)
2. growth or decline of the relevant business communities

Technological factors (D-3)

not applicable

Legal and regulatory factors (D-4)

1. changes to public ordinances regionally that could affect the membership, including interjurisdictional transportation
2. recent cases at law that could have an impact on either the association or its membership

Social and cultural factors (D-5)

not applicable

Competitive Factors (D-6)

1. competition for membership with other associations having overlapping functions or professional coverage
2. competition for membership with chambers of commerce or other general business organizations

Managerial factors (D-7)

1. presence and value of regional societies of association executives

Other factors (D-8)

Figure 2.2. Continued

State environment

Economic and financial factors (E-1)

1. patterns in and projections for state revenues, spending, and appropriations as they affect the membership's business activities
2. projections for funding of existing or new state agencies, programs, or services affecting the membership
3. pending or forthcoming state tax legislation or policies that will affect the association or its membership

Demographic factors (E-2)

1. changing demographics as relates to associations which represent the interests of age, gender, race, etc.

Technological factors (E-3)

1. state university systems' involvement in R & D that is related to the association and its membership

Legal and regulatory factors (E-4)

1. recent legal decisions that could affect the association or its membership
2. activities of state oversight agencies as relates to the fields of interest of the membership
3. changes in state tax codes affecting the association and its membership
4. positions or individuals in the state political arena requiring attention, support, or opposition

Social and cultural factors (E.5)

not applicable

Competitive factors (E-6)

1. for statewide associations, what is the overall performance of the association relative to those in other states

Managerial factors (E-7)

1. offerings in state colleges and universities in skills areas of interest to the association and its membership

Figure 2.2. Continued

National Environment

Economic and financial factors (F-1)
1. trends in relevant key indicators, including inflation, interest rates, business patterns, growth in the GNP, consumer confidence, and patterns of saving and spending, both generally and as relates to the specific areas of interest of the association's membership
2. federal support and assistance for programs of specific interest to the association's membership

Demographic factors (F-2)
1. national trends in population growth, diversity, aging, etc. that will impact the businesses of the association's membership

Technological Factors (F-3)
not applicable

Legal and regulatory factors (F-4)
1. status of current or needed legislation or policies that will affect the specific areas of interest for the association and its members

Social and cultural factors (F-5)
1. general public acceptance of the aims of the association

Competitive factors (F-6)
not applicable

Managerial factors (F-7)
1. the value of ASAE and similar programs to hire, train and retrain, and increase overall professionalism

Other factors (F-8)
not applicable

The Global Environment

Economic and financial factors (G-1)
1. financial stability of countries to which association mem-

Figure 2.2. Continued

bers either directly or indirectly export goods or services or from which they import either goods or services

2. opportunities to initiate or support new import or export programs for the membership
3. relevant economic indicators, including the balance of trade and exchange rates

Demographic factors (G-2)

1. patterns of immigration as it affects members' businesses

Technological factors (G-3)

1. the advance of specific technologies in other countries that may be of interest to the membership

Legal and Regulatory factors (G-4)

1. current and needed federal policies to protect U.S. industry from unfair foreign competitive practices
2. pertinent international laws and practices affecting the association and its members
3. positions or individuals in the national political arena requiring attention, support, or opposition

Social and cultural factors (G-5)

not applicable

Competitive factors (G-6)

1. associations begin to look internationally for members, what is the potential to gain from, or lose to, associations in other countries?

Managerial factors (G-7)

1. ability of members to succeed in other cultures
2. value of ASAE and other programs to hire, train, retrain, and increase staff professionalism

Other factors (G-8)

not applicable

Figure 2.2. Continued

- Most respondents have been a BIA member for at least ten years and have a favorable attitude toward the organization
- The most frequently used BIA services include statistical information, publications, videos, computer programs, and technical assistance
- Companies believe that the most valuable BIA activities are providing technical assistance, serving as government liaison, promoting brick, and keeping members informed about industry developments
- Companies are pleased with BIA's educational opportunities, and would like to see more technical programs on brickwork design and construction offered for both distributors and dealers
- The vast majority of companies believe the merger of the BIA and NABD conventions is good for the industry
- Companies value *BIA News* and find the stories interesting and well written
- *Brick in Architecture, Brick Builder Notes*, and publications for use by members, dealers and local promotion groups are helpful marketing activities
- In addition to the BIA marketing activities directed to architects, the residential builder market should also be targeted
- BIA's promotional activities of clay brick paving should be increased
- Companies place high importance on Engineering and Research's standards, technical publications, and building code services
- The technical issues of greatest concern to members include appearance of brick walls, water penetration, and workmanship of brick walls
- Major problems and opportunities cited by respondents include competing products, lack of qualified masons, and government regulations

This information is invaluable for strategic planners. Subsequent planning and expenditures can be aligned with the areas for which there is a willingness to pay. Conversely, choices between competing demands for scarce resources may become more clear to decision makers with that responsibility.

The detailed analysis that must be performed and which will become the foundation of the strategic plan now has an outline. Using the matrix, planners can examine the identified factors to determine their impact, and goals and objectives will begin to take form.

The Product The results of the environmental scan may be presented in various formats. Generally, the printed document includes a narrative description of the environment, followed by conclusions as to how significant factors may affect the association in the future. The scan may be presented in summary format with detailed analysis of each point.

The accompanying sidebar is extracted from the strategic plan of the American Association of Law Libraries. It summarizes the effects of one factor in their internal environmental scan, Growth and Diversity. The data from the scan, coupled with the conclusions reached about the potential impacts on the future of the association and its membership can provide significant insights to those involved in the next step of the planning process: the development of goals, objectives, and strategies.

Based on this analysis, the planners can identify the opportunities and threats posed by the changes expected in the environment(s). Their next step will be to develop goals, objectives, and strategies to take maximum advantage of the opportunities and to minimize the threats. The reader may find it instructive to regard several examples of association environmental scans. Three such examples may be found in Appendices III, IV, and V. The difference is styles will become immediately apparent. The best style is that which is most comfortable and usable for the individuals and the areas of business involved. Appendix III is extracted from the strategic plan of the American Association of Law Libraries; it presents a complete scan. Appendix IV was taken from the strategic plan of the Printing Industries of America in Alexandria, Virginia, and represents a strong summary format. Appendix V lays out the resulting SWOT analysis that was the result

The American Association of Law Libraries — Internal Scan Factor: Growth and Diversity

AALL has grown rapidly over the last decade. In 1983 membership was just 3454; by 1993 it stood at over 5,000, a 46% increase in ten years. Actually, perhaps reflecting the expansion of the economy...most of the growth took place between 1983 and 1989. In the years since 1989, there was one growth year but, generally speaking, membership has been relatively stable in the 1990s. Over the decade from 1983 to 1993, attendance at the annual meeting has increased even faster than membership, going from 1177, or 36% of the membership,...to 2,264, or 44.8% of the membership...Perhaps more significant than the simple growth in membership is the change in composition of the membership. During the past decade, private law librarians have increased from 25.4% of the membership to 35.1% of the membership in 1993.

Minorities, too, have been participating far more actively in the work of the association in recent years. Although relatively small as a percentage of the overall membership, 235 members of the association have identified themselves as minorities in the 1993-1994 Directory. This number has increased every year since the listing began. Furthermore, there is a Presidential and Executive Board commitment to include minorities in all activities of the association, including appointment to committees. Volunteerism amongst minorities is high, with 19% of all volunteers for committee appointments in 1994-1995...As a result, in 1993-1994, 23 committee

of the environmental scan by the International Association of Financial Planners, located in Atlanta. These examples may help to illustrate to the reader different, yet effective, methods of illustrating the conclusions drawn from the environmental scan.

Once the scan has been completed and the conclusions drawn, it is frequently useful to chart the problems that have been identified and the means by which the associa-

Text continued on page 56

members and four committee chairs were members of minority groups.

Finally, there has been a substantially increased membership from unaffiliated law librarians. In many cases, these are freelance librarians, from law-related associations, and others who don't fit neatly into our type-of-library SIS's. As the association moves into its next stage of development, this category may become increasingly important as it may represent those seeking to bridge traditional library models and roles with newer roles provided by developing network technology. The association needs to be sure that it is meeting the needs of this new kind of legal information professional and it should also take advantage of what they have to offer.

These changes in size, and in the diversity of the membership, have added complexity to the organization at the same time as they have brought a greater diversity of interests and a heightened energy level and vibrancy concerning the future. In recent years, more elected leadership positions than ever before have been occupied by librarians other than academic law librarians. Programs sponsored by the Special Interest Sections and the Caucuses demonstrate the wide range of interests of our members. Minority law librarians have promoted law librarianship and AALL at a national conference of African-American librarians. This diversity is to be prized and encouraged as we strive to keep the association relevant to the newest generation of law librarians.

tion may be able to reverse those fortunes and, given time and resources, convert them into opportunities for the association and its membership. Such a (fictional) characterization is demonstrated in the table below. Again, standard formats for such exercises are not generally advisable. What makes sense in any given situation and with a given set of players is quite simply what makes sense. It may change over time, or as the key members involved change. It will almost certainly change from one association to the next.

The lessons extracted from environmental scanning form the basis for decisions about goals and objectives. The process demonstrates the usefulness of organizing information in a structured way. One such structure is demonstrated in Figure 2.3 (right), using fictitious analyses.

Thus structured and abbreviated, the lessons culled from the environmental scan can more easily be translated into goals and objectives. These will be actions through which the association will endeavor to maximize its strengths and take advantage of its opportunities, while minimizing threats and overcoming its weaknesses.

1. Kami, Kami Strategic Assumptions, p. 2.
2. Thomas J. Peters and Robert H. Waterman,Jr., In Search of Excellence (New York: Harper and Row Publishers, 1982), p. 285
3. Ibid.
4. Benjamin B. Tregoe and Peter M. Tobia, "An Action Oriented Approach to Strategy," *Journal of Business Strategy*, 11, no. 16 (January/February 1990)

Problems	Related Opportunities
1. Declining revenues	1. Potential sources of relief
a. competition for membership is increasing from international associations	a. enhanced opportunities for co-sponsored programs
b. member attendance at programs is decreasing	b. impetus provided to re-assess member needs and interests
c. foundation/grant support is being scaled back	c. no opportunities identified
d. advertising support for publications has remained static as costs have increased	d. technology sufficient to produce more publications in-house to reduce expenses
2. Legislative issues	2. Potential community support
a. pending bill will significantly increase oversight of industry by state agencies	a. recent debates in legislature have identified an industry champion
b. community support of association at headquarters location remains uncertain/ mixed	b. no true opposition is active; local unemployment rate is above average for the state
3. Internal competition	3. Possible solutions
a. long-standing (volunteer) leadership being challenged by younger members	a. opportunities exist to increase roles and output of committees
b. competition amongst senior staff for leadership responsibilities	b. talent of staff creates potential to provide new services/programs

Figure 2.3

Chapter 3

The Strategic Plan: Programs

Once an association has collectively examined the factors that may affect its future, it needs to decide where it wants to be in the years ahead and determine how to get there. Thus, the next steps in strategic planning are setting goals and objectives, devising strategies, and creating implementation plans. At this point, the time frame for planning begins to shorten. While the environmental scan may look ahead for a period of years, it is best to set a time of one year for the steps outlined in this chapter.

Goals

Goals are generalized statements of where an organization wants to be at some future time. For purposes of this chapter, the goals will be generalized statements of where the association wishes to be in twelve months. Goals tend to be relatively few in number, concise yet not specific, and non-quantitative. Again, it may be a productive exercise to review the goal statements of other associations' plans. Several sets follow:

National Center for Missing and Exploited Children

- find missing children
- prevent child victimization and exploitation
- ensure financial survival
- create organizational awareness

National Association of College Stores

- encourage and enable college stores to connect with their key stakeholders
- forge connections between NACS and its key stakeholders
- strengthen NACS and its ability to serve members
- become the hub for information, knowledge and research about the industry
- provide education, products and services to support members' business and service objectives and to help stores compete effectively
- act as the national voice for college stores

American Consulting Engineers Council

- enhance and expand market opportunities for member firms
- assist member firms to improve their business ability, upgrade the quality of their services, and achieve their financial goals
- advocate improvement of the business environment of member firms
- continuously improve the professional and business image of member firms and the association
- support a flexible and interactive association, and improve its value to the members in a changing market

American Machine Tool Distributors' Association

- to provide effective education programs for members to increase the knowledge and competency of their personnel

- to effectively communicate to members to ensure thorough dialogue between the association and the membership
- to represent the majority of marketers of manufacturing technology through growth of the association by actively seeking all qualified companies for membership
- AMTDA and AMT will be the definitive resource of marketing data by collection and dissemination of industry statistics
- to effectively communicate with external organizations through dialogue with manufacturers, customers, media, government, and allied associations
- to increase the effectiveness of trade shows by making shows more productive for members and customers
- to provide effective group services by utilizing the collective value of the membership

Northern Virginia Technology Council

- deliver programs and services to add value to NVTC membership
- advocate a statutory, regulatory, financial and workforce infrastructure necessary for the development, growth and international competitiveness of the technology industry
- establish NVTC as the communications nexus for technology businesses in northern Virginia in order to foster cooperative working relationships and serve as a common meeting ground
- act as a catalyst for regional economic and community development through technology applications and appropriate partnerships
- create and maintain an organizational infrastructure of professionals and members to support the NVTC mission

National Council of Teachers of Mathematics

- to foster excellence in school mathematics curricula, instruction, and assessment
- to create a climate throughout the Council that demonstrates a respect for, and valuing of, diversity
- to stimulate students' interests, confidence, and learning in mathematics
- to strengthen leadership in, and service to, mathematics education
- to foster excellence in professional development throughout the preparation and the career of teachers of mathematics at all levels, pre-K through college
- to encourage research and development in mathematics education
- to identify and influence the forces of change affecting mathematics education

Further delineation provides the sum and substance of these goals. An organization's goals may change from time to time, but it is not unusual for change to occur slowly and in small increments. Goals are usually very general in nature and should be attainable yet sufficiently ambitious to make an organization and its people stretch. If a goal is too ambitious, there will be frustration; if it is too lenient, less than maximal performance is tolerated. Establishing a few goals is a more productive exercise than developing many. Often, it is useful to incorporate some goals that are readily achievable, thereby ensuring at least partial success. Goals will often become evident after the environmental scan is completed and the resulting lessons are properly structured.

Some additional examples of goal statements are listed in Figure 3.1, together with the relevant cells on the environmental scanning matrix. Although these goals are few in number, each represents an ambitious target for one year and each represents a series of programs and activities. Finally, each represents problems and opportunities. Each will require an association to apply the strengths of the organization and improve upon its weaknesses.

At the end of the year, an association's leadership will be able to determine the association's success in a general way by judging whether these goals have been achieved.

Objectives

Objectives are the specific, measurable targets set for each goal. They are short-term in nature and there are, typically, several for each goal. Objectives are measurable and constitute the means by which a plan's success can be gauged.

Often, a plan's objectives are broken into sub- and sub-sub-objectives, depending on the desired level of detail in the plan. Objectives must be stated as succinctly as possible and be immediately understandable.

Like the goals, the objectives will draw upon data from numerous cells in the strategic planning matrix. As an example, the first goal in Figure 3.1 is repeated in Figure 3.2 with examples of several objectives and the environmental scanning matrix cells from which data might be taken to structure such objectives. A consistent pattern of numbers and letters to identify goals, objectives, and sub-objectives facilitates later reference.

Of course, it is possible for different individuals to view the same data and arrive at different goals and objectives. Different approaches are not necessarily right or wrong; they simply reflect the diversity of values and approaches among associations.

Again, it is often useful to observe how others do things. Several sets of objectives can be found in the appendices of this book. Some are very detailed and others are not.

Text continued on page 66

Goals	Environmental Factors (from scanning matrix)	
I. Identify means of increasing revenues without a dues increase	cell A-1	Internal environment, economic and financial factors
	cell A-2	Internal environment, demographic factors
	cell F-1	National environment, economic and financial factors
	cell B-6	Association management environment, competitive factors
	cell G-6	Global environment, competitive factors
II. Increase membership participation/attendance in programs	cell A-1	Internal environment, economic and financial factors
	cell A-2	Internal environment, demographic factors
	cell A-5	Internal environment, social and cultural factors
	cell B-2	Association management environment, demographic factors
	cell B-6	Association management environment, competitive factors
III. Defeat State Legislative Bill Number 421	cell E-2	State environment, demographic factors
	cell E-4	State environment, legal and regulatory factors
	cell E-5	State environment, social and cultural factors
	cell A-4	Internal environment, legal and regulatory factors

Figure 3.1. Goals and relevant factors from the environmental scanning matrix

	cell A-5 Internal environment, social and cultural factors cell B-1 Association management environment, economic and financial factors cell B-4 Association management environment cell E-1 State environment, economic and financial factors
IV. Solidify community support for the association at the headquarters location	cell A-2 Internal environment, demographic factors cell C-1 Local environment, economic and financial factors cell C-2 Local environment, demographic factors cell C-5 Local environment, social and cultural factors cell D-2 Regional environment, demographic factors cell D-5 Regional environment, social and cultural factors
V. Create leadership opportunities for younger members while retaining the experienced leadership of the association	cell A-2 Internal environment, demographic factors cell A-5 Internal environment, social and cultural factors cell A-6 Internal environment, competitive factors cell B-2 Association management environment, demographic factors cell B-5 Association management environment, social and cultural factors

Figure 3.1 Continued

The following array of objectives is extracted from the first several goals in the long-range plan of the Restaurant Association of Metropolitan Washington, located in Tysons Corner, Virginia.

These objectives represent a good illustration of very succinct objectives supporting the various goals. Often,

Goal 1: To develop and implement educational and training opportunities serving the food service industry in the Metropolitan Washington area.

Objectives:

- foster and upgrade professional competency at all levels
- provide income-producing training programs
- act as a focal point for advice and dissemination of professional development materials
- support and develop relationship with area high schools, institutions of higher learning, and community-based training programs
- encourage and support post-secondary education for the study of the hospitality industry

Goal 2: Increase the association membership to represent 33% of the food service establishments and units of operation in the region.

Objectives:

- develop an aggressive schedule and marketing plan to attract commercial and non-commercial food service operators and no more than 250 associate memberships
- pursue dual membership with NRA-affiliated associations to support national and regional membership issues
- create a simplified dues structure
- the immediate Past President will chair the Membership Committee and at least two Directors will be assigned by the Association President

Goal 3: To provide a comprehensive membership benefit package in order to maximize the value of the membership

brevity in the written plan is productive as an effective tool for staff-level planning and programming. The detail and measurability will be found in the organization's operating plans and budget. Again, different approaches can be more or less successful in different organizations and at different times. No one method is best or right; it is

and to attract new members to the organization.

Objectives:

- provide quality publications and timely communications with members
- provide a Buyer's Guide of associate members
- provide educational support to include seminars, in-house training and certification programs
- develop services that provide value and savings for the membership

Goal 4: Establish the show into a strong regional convention/exposition (attendance 15,000+).

Objectives:

- increase show participation by government-related purchasers/buyers
- focus on exhibitors of non-food products
- solicit companies that provide support services to the food service industry
- design programs that will stimulate and increase participation

Goal 5: Maintain and monitor political issues that affect the hospitality industry.

Objectives:

- pursue changes in legislation and regulations that affect the hospitality industry
- develop and maintain communications with government and regulatory officials
- maintain a membership network to facilitate grassroots lobbying
- maintain a political action committee (PAC) that supports hospitality industry goals

not a one-size-fits-all practice.

Strategies

Strategies are the step-by-step means by which an organization reaches its objectives. They typically constitute programs, events, operations, and projects for the organization to accomplish its objectives. In short, they are the action steps.

Typically, each objective under each goal will have a series of such strategies. These strategies may range from complex projects to one-time, easily performed tasks. The goals and objectives indicate where the organization wants to go and what it expects to accomplish, and the strategies tell how.

Goal V. Create leadership opportunities for younger members while retaining the experienced leadership of the association. (environmental scanning matrix cells A-2, A-5, A-6, B-2, B-5)

Objective V,a Assess member preferences for new program emphases by June 1 (environmental scanning matrix cells A-2, A-4, A-5, A-6, A-7, B-1, B-3, B-4, B-6, B-7)

Objective V,b Determine member satisfaction with existing programs and services by June 1 (environmental scanning matrix cells A-1, A-2, A-3, A-4, A-5, A-7, B-6)

Objective V,c Establish a task force to review existing and desired/potential new programs and committee structure by September 1 (environmental scanning matrix cells A-2, A-5, A-6, A-7)

Objective V,d Create up to three new programs (and relevant committees) this year with new leadership opportunities (environmental scanning matrix cells A-1, A-2, A-5,A-6, A-7)

Figure 3.2. Objectives supporting a strategic planning goal, with references to cells in the environmental scanning matrix

Goals and strategies can touch any functional area in an association. Peter Drucker suggests eight areas in which objectives and strategies may be set: "marketing, innovation, human organization, financial resources, physical resources, productivity, social responsibilities, and profit."[1] This is a particularly instructive list for associations. Frequently, strategies will be described in detail and will be defined in sub-strategies and even sub-sub-strategies. Obviously, such detail becomes more important as the tasks to be performed become more complex.

The strategies or action steps for two of the objectives for Goal I in Figure 3.2 are spelled out in Figure 3.3. These strategies constitute programs and projects consistent with, and responsive to, the lessons extracted from the environmental scan. It is at this point in any plan that planners and managers can get so excited about new project development that they overlook or discount environmental factors that can ensure success or impede progress.

Frequently, plans result in the identification of strategies which are important and desirable for the association, but for which sufficient resources are not available. Tabling the concept until resources can be found, or discarding the idea, are feasible options. However, another approach is to identify new resources for projects and programs. If that is the approach that the association elects to pursue, then strategies must be developed in the plan to accomplish the objective of resource identification and acquisition.

Figure 3.3 represents one array of strategies. It is possible that other strategies, even contrary strategies, could also be consistent with the environmental scan and be successful. Strategies are not necessarily either right or wrong but simply one planner's reaction to the environmental factors projected to affect the organization in the future.

Because it is frequently useful to view actual strategic plans, two strong examples of lists of goals, objectives, and strategies are provided in Appendices VI, VII, VIII, and IX. These goals, objectives, and strategies were developed by the Academy of General Dentistry, by the Door and Hardware Institute, and by the National Center for Missing and Exploited Children in Arlington, Virginia. They may be studied to observe the manner in which the goals, objectives, and strategies taken from the plans of these three associations are arrayed and how each is both consistent with the others and draws a clear path to the vision of the future being sought by those groups.

These examples of goals, objectives, and strategies may seem ambitious. It is important to state in the plan

Objective V, a Assess member preferences for new program emphasis by June 1 (environmental scanning matrix cells A-2, A-4, A-5, A-6, B-1, B-3, B-4, B-6, B-7)

Strategies (or action steps):

1. decide on process, outcomes; proceed to the Board of Directors in late June/early July
2. appoint committee and chairman to conduct review and issue charge by August 1
3. review process and identify non-staff resources by August 15
4. committee membership solicited by September 1
5. committee reviews issues and data by December 1
6. survey instrument completed by January 2
7. survey completed by February 15
8. committee reviews survey results and reaches conclusions by April 1
9. report submitted to Board of Directors by May 1
10. recommendations that are accepted are priced and implemented by June 1

Figure 3-3. Strategies for two objectives

what can be accomplished in the first twelve-month cycle. For example, creating the proposal teams, preparing the necessary materials, and identifying funding sources may be sufficient for a plan if it is a start-up effort. Solicitation can be incorporated into subsequent planning cycles. This will vary for individual associations.

It is also important that strategies be supported by adequate personnel and budgetary resources. If they are not, their inclusion in the plan can do more harm than good, leading to discouragement and internal conflicts.

One of the difficult tasks of management is the allocation of scarce resources among competing demands, suggesting a zero sum scenario in which a gain by one pro-

Objective VII, c Support the passage of United States Senate Bill No. 1524 during the current Congress (environmental scanning matrix cells A-3, A-4, A-6, B-4, B-7, E-2, E-4, F-1, F-2, F-4, F-5, F-6, F-7, G-1, G-4, G-7)

Strategies (or action steps):
1. notify membership of the issue, the association's position, and plans to address the matter by March 1
2. Chairman, Executive Office, legislative staff and committee identify process, participants, and roles at the April meetings
3. white paper completed to illustrate the potential benefits and costs of the legislation by May 31
4. key legislators identified by May 31
5. stakeholder map generated to determine the best means of having input to legislative decision makers by May 31
6. support campaign developed and implemented, including special events, public service announcements, advertising, and/or a speakers bureau by June 30
7. newsletter developed to keep members informed and involved with local legislative delegation

Figure 3-3. Continued

gram represents the lack of a gain or loss by another. These competing demands should be negotiated during the planning process. Resource limitations should be identified and decision points laid out for those who must make the difficult decisions to proceed in some directions and not in others. For each choice, the relative costs and benefits should be identified.

These decisions are best communicated to the affected and interested parties when they have been made with the most complete understanding of circumstances and consequences and arrived at and publicized early. When these difficult decisions have been made and announced, the plan can be finalized, and those responsible for implementing the resulting programs can begin to do so.

It is timely here to mention the special nature of cooperation and competition in the field of association management. Businesses compete with one another for finite markets or to develop goods or services which will be sufficiently attractive to create new markets. Associations may also compete in some ways. Associations may compete with one another for membership and the available budgeted amounts for dues and time. This will be especially so in associations that have related aims or which are in close proximity to one another. Associations may compete as well for conference attendees and advertising for their publications. The business instinct to protect proprietary information, as expressed in the rhetorical question "Does Macy's tell Gimbel's?" may not be the response of an association executive. But, in general, there may be no reason for one association not to share its successes with another. In fact, those who are members of one association board are likely to be involved with others as well.

Many of the needs that an association will address over time, then, are not unique. Often, there will be substantial information available on models that have been employed elsewhere. The association planner should be aware not only of needs and available resources, but also of as many alternative program strategies as possible.

Implementation plans

The implementation plan takes the strategic planning process to the level of individuals. Prior to this, in setting goals, objectives, and strategies, the planning has related to the association, as a unit, and its needs and programs. The implementation plan assigns specific responsibilities for those programs and strategies. At this point, individuals and groups within the organization are drawn into the plan.

The implementation plan forms the basis for personnel assignments and performance measures. Ultimately, promotions, demotions, dismissals, and other personnel actions can result from individuals' abilities to carry out successfully the assignments of the implementation plan. Witness the following description of the great importance placed on the plan in relation to the performance measurement of the individual staff in just one organization. The chief executive officer of the Bethesda, Maryland-based Federation of American Societies for Experimental Biology (FASEB) wrote:

> An important concern that arose in relation to the compensation management system as it was originally installed, was the subjective and reactive nature of the performance appraisal. For this reason, we subsequently designed and implemented a performance management system. This system is not directly linked to compensation management, but adds an objective dimension to the appraisal of performance. The performance management system is designed to achieve four objectives. First, the performance objectives are defined prospectively at the start of the appraisal period. Second, the staff member and the supervisor consult and agree on the definition of objectives and the criteria for their achievement. Next, the supervisor is expected to provide regular feedback on performance as it relates

to the agreed on objectives and, in defining objectives, staff are expected to integrate their personal objectives with concepts of departmental goals and the mission of the organization.

Thus, it is critical that this section of the plan, perhaps more than any other, receive commitment from all managers, workers, and volunteers throughout the involved association.

Figure 3.4 is an example of an implementation plan for the ten strategies supporting the first objective outlined in Figure 3.3. Obviously, the implementation plan for all of the goals, objectives, and strategies in a plan will be lengthy. Equally obvious is the fact that there will be different options available; the figure shows just one possible set of plans. And, of course, the plans will be much more detailed.

Implementation plans in actual association documents often list the strategies and then list the corresponding member, staff person, or committee with the primary responsibility for that effort. This style is shown in Figure 3.5, which builds on the goals, objectives, and strategies developed earlier in the chapter.

Another format is demonstrated in Appendix X, which shows the implementation plan which has been derived from the goals, objectives, and strategies of the National Head Start Association, housed in Alexandria, Virginia.

After the planning document has been reviewed and approved, and before it is put into operation, the implementation plan serves another purpose. Since it assigns duties and responsibilities to individuals and organizational units, it provides a basis for developing performance standards. By linking organizational and individual performance criteria, evaluations, and rewards to the

Text continues on page79

Goal V Create leadership opportunities for younger members while retaining the experienced leadership of the association (environmental scanning matrix cells A-2, A-5, A-6, B-2, B-5)

Objective V, a Assess member preferences for new program emphases by June 1

Strategy 1. Decide on process and outcomes; present to the Board of Directors in late June/early July

Implementation plan:

a. Department heads propose outcomes, etc. to Executive Officer
b. Executive Officer reviews proposal with Chairman of the Board
c. Communications Director notifies membership of the process and forwards draft proposal to the full Board
d. Chairman and Board approve the proposal

Strategy 2. Appoint committee and chairman to conduct review and issue charge by August 1

Implementation plan:

a. Chairman of the board appoints a committee chairman
b. Committee chairman designates other board members to participate
c. Executive officer assigns staff resources to support the committee
d. Staff liaison discusses process and budget needs with executive officer and chief financial officer

Strategy 3. Review process and identify non-staff resources by August 15

Implementation plan:

a. executive officer meets with committee chairman to identify process and non-staff resources
b. executive officer and committee staff prepare budget requirements

Figure 3.4. Part of an implementation plan

c. Chief financial officer ensures funding availability
d. Chairman outlines committee schedule, staff responsibilities, and procedural steps

Strategy 4. Committee membership solicited by September 1

Implementation plan:

a. Chairman specifies categories of members for committee as well as specific persons
b. Executive officer extends invitations to specific individuals
c. Staff liaison issues a general invitation to members or groups to participate
d. Executive officer submits final list to the committee chairman
e. Committee chairman submits final list to the chairman of the board

Strategy 5. Committee review issues and data by December 1

Implementation plan:

a. Committee identifies research needs to staff liaison
b. Legal counsel and executive officer provide detail of issues confronting the association and the membership
c. Research director provides statistical information relating to specific issues

Strategy 6. Survey instrument completed by January 2

Implementation plan:

a. Committee determines what issues and questions should be addressed by the membership
b. Staff liaison directs research director to draft survey instrument
c. Executive officer and legal counsel review survey instrument
d. Staff liaison presents survey instrument to the committee

Figure 3.4. Continued

Strategy 7. Survey completed by February 15

Implementation plan:

a. Communications division processes survey forms
b. Research division compiles and summarizes responses
c. Committee liaison presents survey results to the executive officer
d. Committee liaison presents survey results to the committee chairman

Strategy 8. Committee reviews survey results and reaches conclusions by April 1

Implementation plan:

a. Committee members review final tabulations and staff recommendations
b. Committee reaches final conclusions
c. Staff liaison drafts final report
d. Committee chairman reviews and approves the report

Strategy 9. Report submitted to the Board of Directors by May 1

Implementation plan:

a. Executive officer, committee chairman, and committee liaison review final draft
b. Committee chairman presents final report to the Board of Directors for review and approval
c. Conclusions are reported to the membership by the Communications Director

Strategy 10. Recommendations that are accepted are priced and implemented by June 1

Implementation plan:

a. Executive Officer reviews discussions with Chief Financial Officer, committee liaison, and senior staff
b. The necessary resources are identified
c. A reporting schedule and format are prepared by the Executive Officer
d. Programs are implemented by the relevant divisions

Figure 3.4. Continued

Goal V Create leadership opportunities for younger members while retaining the experienced leadership of the association.

Objective V, a Assess member preferences for new program preferences by June 1.

Strategy #	Strategy	Primary Responsibility	Support Responsibility
1	decide on process and outcomes, report to Board of Directors	Executive Officer	Chairman/Board
2	appoint committee and chairman to conduct review and issue charge	Chairman of Board committee chairman	Executive Officer Staff liaison Chief Financial Officer
3	identify process and non-staff resources	committee chairman executive officer	Chief Financial Officer staff liaison
4	solicit committee membership	committee chairman	Executive Officer staff liaison
5	committee reviews issues and data	staff liaison	Executive Officer Legal Counsel Research Director
6	print survey instrument	committee chairman	staff liaison Research Director Executive Officer Legal Counsel
7	complete survey	staff liaison	Communications Director Research Director
8	committee reviews survey results and reaches conclusions	committee chairman	staff liaison
9	report submitted to the Board of Directors	committee chairman	Executive Officer staff liaison
10	recommendations that are accepted are priced and implemented	Executive Officer	staff liaison Chief Financial Officer senior staff

Figure 3.5. Assignment of responsibilities for strategies

implementation plan, the planners can pin a measure of incremental understanding, appreciation, and support for the plan and its goals, objectives, and strategies.

Finally, the goals, objectives, and strategies provide the association with an outline of programs, services, facilities, and staff to be funded over the period of the plan. Thus, it is a blueprint for the budgeting process. Once approved, plans will dictate the allocation of finite resources. As noted earlier, funding one set of strategies will, more often than not, result in reductions in, or elimination of, funding for others.

Strategic planners must be aware of the available resources and construct the plan accordingly. The plan may also identify programs or service areas that are priorities for increases, should other funds or other resources become available.

Frequently, implementation plans will highlight recommended services and programs in a tiered approach. This permits the decision makers to have the benefit of the planner's recommended levels of service within the confines of existing resources and to select the expansion of one strategy over another. If such options are not indicated, the decision makers have no choice but to approve the plan as submitted or conduct further study. The best plans are those which provide the clearest set of alternatives and the most flexible format for making those difficult decisions from competing options.

Once an association is prepared to put the plan into action, it must ensure that the plan is monitored, the performance is measured, and the lessons learned are incorporated in this as well as future planning efforts.

1. Peter Drucker, Management (New York: Harper and Row Publishers, 1973), p. 100.

Chapter 4

The Strategic Plan: Review

The implementation plan is a blueprint for action by the association during the coming year. As the year goes by, managers and supervisors need some means of determining how successfully the plan is being carried out and some guidance on what to do if the plan is not proceeding as expected. Controls, feedback mechanisms, and contingency plans are all tools that can help those who are responsible for monitoring and correcting the organizations performance.

Controls

Controls are mechanisms to help managers and decision makers gauge the performance of an organization in relation to planned or projected outcomes. Often called *performance measures*, they provide a means for determining whether the organization is on track and, if it is not, for identifying and implementing corrective actions.

If a review of performance measures indicates that the organization is achieving its targets, decision makers may decide to maintain the current level of effort or to increase the targets, thereby making the organization "stretch." If performance is below expectations, it may be that steps must be taken to improve output, or it may be that the plan was unrealistic and requires adjustment.

Attention to control mechanisms in the strategic planning process is required at three distinct times: (1) before the plan is implemented, (2) during the period of operations under the plan, and (3) after the plan cycle has been completed.

Prior to implementation and as a part of the written document, strategic planners must identify benchmarks that indicate progress toward the plan's objectives. They must then ensure that the organization prepares itself to collect mechanically the necessary performance data, to analyze the data, and to ensure that actions are taken to correct any problems or to take advantage of any opportunities suggested by the data.

During the implementation of the plan, these mechanisms must be activated. Individuals and departments need to keep and submit records of activities and progress; supervisors need to appraise the performance of employees; analysts need to monitor performance based on this information. This process will enable those responsible to refine operations as they are under way and react to changes in circumstances or new information.

After the period of time covered by the plan, the control mechanisms will provide the basis for final reports of actual performance compared with planned objectives. Such reports are instructive, as they show the achievements and shortcomings of the organization. The lessons learned through these reports should become part of the organization's body of knowledge to be incorporated into future planning efforts.

In most strategic plans, the measurements suggested

by the objectives are actions accompanied by either dates or numeric targets. The latter may be expressed as numbers or as percentages:

- submit four proposals by December 31
- complete fifteen files per month
- provide service to 80 members
- increase revenues by 4%
- decrease complaints by 2%
- increase seminar attendance by 5%

The simplest control mechanism may be a calendar or a "tickler" file to ensure that progress is checked in a timely manner. Often, complex control sheets, journal entries, and computerized management information systems are required. If complex systems are to be used, they must be in place at the beginning of the cycle of program operations.

Feedback

Feedback loops are well known modeling concepts in many disciplines. The feedback loop is used in strategic planning to ensure that the lessons learned in the current strategic planning cycle are built into future cycles. Such lessons may be explanations for successes and failures, or may indicate the level of effectiveness in reading and assembling relevant environmental factors.

Some organizations build the responsibility for feedback directly into the implementation plan. If this is not the case, a brief special section in the planning document is often used to guarantee that one or more individuals are assigned the task of providing input from one year's plan into ensuing cycles. The text for such a section might be something like this:

Soon after the completion of the period for which

this plan is operational, the association manager will call a meeting of such individuals as he or she may deem appropriate. The purpose of this and any subsequent meetings will be to determine the lessons learned in the annual planning exercise and in the course of implementing the plan, and to ensure that they become a part of the knowledge base incorporated into future planning and operating efforts. This will include an assessment of both effective and ineffective techniques. It will also include an analysis of performance levels that can reasonably be expected in certain areas under stated conditions. These findings will be shared with the association Board of Directors and incorporated in the ongoing planning process.

While this simple statement may seem self-evident or unnecessary, it is a good opportunity for a senior executive to endorse the concept of strategic planning and to ensure that there is improvement in the method from one year to the next.

In this context, it is important to document the performance of existing programs. The phrase "documenting program performance" may also be read "justifying program continuation." The decision to continue an existing program is based on three things: demonstrating an ongoing need for the program, illustrating the success of the program in response to the expressed need, and analyzing the value of responding to the need with a given level of resources.

Thus, if a plan incorporates the continuation of specific services or programs, officials must not only be shown that the need is real and the resources well spent; they must also be convinced that the proposed array of services is the one most likely to address the need most acceptably and inexpensively. Similarly, if new programs or services are proposed to replace existing ones, the ineffectiveness or inefficiency of the latter must be demonstrated.

One role of the strategic planner, then, must be to ensure that adequate systems measure the effectiveness of programs and services in meeting the needs for which the operation was first established. This requires thorough examination of both the needs and the program objectives.

It is incumbent upon the association strategic planner to ensure that reliable data are available to demonstrate the need for programs and services, to allow decision makers to make informed judgments, to permit administrators to fine-tune programs and services, and to understand whether the ongoing effort is effective in resolving the situation in the best way possible with the least possible expenditure of scarce resources.

Contingency plans

Contingency plans address "what if?" situations:

- What if legislation is introduced that could seriously damage our members' ability to compete, succeed, or stay in business?
- What if membership declines so dramatically that all programs have to be either eliminated or seriously reduced, including some of which are essential elements of the association's services?
- What if the association sponsors a conference and there is insufficient attendance to break even?
- what if the search to find a cure for the illness we exist to combat is suddenly successful?
- What if the chairman of the board or the president unexpectedly dies (especially in a smaller association)?

In its contingency planning, an organization identifies events that are not predictable from the environmental scan and are not anticipated in the goals, objectives, and strategies.

Each contingency is accompanied by an implementation plan to be used "in the event." Thus, managers can react quickly rather than beginning to deliberate at the eleventh hour.

In the contingency situations listed above, the association could, for example, find itself and the membership confronting an unexpected piece of legislation that could have effects of disastrous proportions. Planners must have alternatives of both short- and long-term solutions. In the short-term these may entail appeals to the "champions" of their industry in the legislature. Long-term solutions might involve invigorated communications plans to create grass roots support for the preferred position, or in support of the association and its aims in general.

In a business contingency plan, the "what if" question might relate to a failure to gain an acceptable return on an investment, or to penetrate a new market. Contingency plans tend to be different for associations which are not solely concerned with profit. An association's contingency plans may, however, address membership dues and other sources of revenues, which affect the ability to provide services, or fluctuations in the prime rate, which affect the ability to borrow money or conduct programs. Contingency plans for the association may also need to take account of periodic changes in organizational leadership.

Contingency plans may need to be implemented for several reasons. It could be that one or more environmental factors were inaccurately assessed in the planning process. Or it could be that an environmental factor changed substantially, requiring a change in part of the plan. Frequently such occurrences will be identified early through the control system, allowing timely modification to the plan and programs.

These examples illustrate the value of contingency

planning. It enables associations to react swiftly, maintain member confidence, and correct problems. In short, the contingency plan prepares an organization for disaster rather than permitting the disaster to take control. Such plans can be implemented in reaction to early warnings.

Although contingency plans often address unwanted or negative eventualities, there is much to be derived from planning for positive occurrences as well. For a business, positive "what if's" may relate to an unexpected sales volume, a competitor leaving the field, or the development of a breakthrough product.

For associations, contingency planning for positive occurrences tends to be done on an issue-by-issue or an event-by-event basis. For example, a publication may be extraordinarily effective in attracting advertising support, thereby generating revenue with which to conduct additional activities.

For contingency situations that cannot be anticipated and planned for, some organizations establish standard emergency response or quick response teams which convene immediately in the case of any crisis to chart the best possible reaction on the spot. This, too, is a form of contingency planning. It addresses the question, "What if something happens that we haven't anticipated?" Emergency response teams may be composed of the chief elected officer, the chief financial officer, the chief administrative officer, the public information officer, and others as appropriate to the organization and the situation.

For associations, there are many possible "what if's" to anticipate. Over time, most organizations develop contingency plans, often in great detail. For whatever reason an association prepares for contingency situations, the mere practice of anticipation can result in better response and resolution of unanticipated problems and opportunities.

Chapter 5

Organizational Considerations

In order for strategic planning to be effective, it must be fully accepted at the senior-most levels and integrated into the association as both a product and a process. Several organizational considerations deserve mention in this regard: the development of strategic thinking, the effectiveness of the organization's decision making style, the organization's sensitivity to ethics, and the role of human resources functions in implementation of the plan.

Strategic thinking

The creation of a strategic mindset is vital in the strategic planning process. There must evolve a type of strategic thinking that is directed from the very top of the association and that focuses constantly on issues affecting the future of the membership and the ability of its association to be successful.

Strategic thinking in any organization generally evolves with the strategic planning process over the years.

Organizations whose strategic planning processes are in an early stage of development tend to be oriented to "number crunching. "As the planning process evolves, changes occur: the planning increasingly focuses on issues instead of numbers, and the members of the organization increasingly accept and comply with the planning process and the plan itself. Perhaps most important, the role of the senior managers of the organization changes.

Strategic planning literature and research suggest that the primary role of senior executives is strategic thinking. The higher one moves in organizational management, the greater the amount of time that should be devoted to strategic planning, with a predominant orientation toward future issues. At the same time, mid-level and front-line managers should devote a greater share of their time to implementing plans, with some time devoted to strategic thinking.

So important is the "mindset" to ensure that planning is embraced as a concept and facilitated as a process that many strategic planners spell out what is expected in the plan itself. Often, the explanations appear elementary. Typically, these are the basic principles by which we are taught to conduct discussions:

1. Respect the opinions of others, regardless of rank
2. Allow others to speak, regardless of one's own position
3. Encourage those who are reluctant to participate
4. Support each member of the group to encourage teamwork and pursue a common purpose
5. Promote compromise

Strategic thinking, however important, is not an easy skill to develop or to exercise. The decision making process is both constant and constantly changing. It may sound fine to suggest that strategic thought and reflection on the future are deserving of an association executive's or any senior manager's time. It is entirely different actually to find the time to practice them.

Further, strategic decisions often require a great deal of courage. Business as usual is easy, and subsequent failures can be attributed to the mere continuation of past practices. But to risk the survival or success of entire programs, the well-being of members, and one's reputation on decisions to move in new directions, can require both personal and organizational courage.

Finally, decisions and decision making styles are necessarily unique to organizations, situations, and the individuals involved. Still, some decision making styles can be more effective than others in the strategic planning process. This influence on both product and process will be addressed in the next section.

Decision making styles

There are several categories of decision making styles. Two items should be considered in relation to strategic planning and decision making in associations: first, the direction of the decision making process (top-down or bottom-up) and second, the advantages and disadvantages of group decision making.

Top-down versus bottom-up decision making Decision making in an organization can flow from the top down or from the bottom up. As the name implies, the top-down approach begins with senior management. This may be the senior, or it may be one or more of the organization's leaders who have been made responsible for planning. Decisions made at this level flow downward through the organization. Thus, the chairman of the board or the executive vice president (or his or her designee) might set the general tone and then develop an outline with department heads' involvement. Subsequent input from other employees may be sought, subject to the approval of those at the top of the organizational pyramid. This approach tends to prevail in organizations where initial efforts at strategic planning are beginning to replace more intuitive styles of decision making in which leaders may either consciously or unconsciously have imposed their decisions on the organization.

In the bottom-up approach, information, ideas, and other input rise freely from the lower or middle ranks of an organization to senior leadership for consideration. This method takes advantage of the collective experience of those who actually implement plans and programs. Data and relevant input are sifted and passed along to be incorporated in decisions made by senior managers.

There are, of course, many variations on these themes. Strategic decisions may be developed using a method which combines the best aspects of the bottom-up and top-down approaches, after which the proposals are merged for final review at the senior level.

Another variation —team strategic decision making— has become popular. It has the advantage of permitting the planning team to represent all levels in the organization in one consistent process.

No one approach is necessarily right or wrong for every organization or for any organization at every point in time. Associations must decide what style works best for them at the current time with the current participants and constraints.

The top-down and bottom-up approaches both have distinct advantages and disadvantages in the strategic planning process. The top-down approach may not take into full account the experiences of those on the front line. Decisions made by senior executives are either made without that intelligence or must rely on reports, printouts, or other analyses. This explains why many plans that result from a top-down style are dominated by statistical data, sometimes at the expense of analyses of relevant issues.

Another drawback to the top-down approach is the implication to those in the organization who are not involved that they have no input into such decisions and that their collective experience does not merit consideration.

The bottom-up approach seems to be more egalitarian and democratic. Yet it too has drawbacks. Senior management is responsible for difficult decisions; bottom-up styles vest a great deal of power in those who will be the least responsible for the consequences of decisions and who are least likely to have a global view of the organization's future.

The extension of this problem is that, as recommendations rise from the bottom, each organizational unit and each committee contributes separately to the plan. Strategic planners must beware not to permit the total projected plan of the organization to be the mere sum of input from its various parts.

It is most advantageous for the strategic planning decision making process to include both the view from the top of where to go and the view from the bottom of how best to get there. Recognition of this need has led to a greater reliance on the group style, which incorporates various levels of the organization in the decision making process. But even this approach has disadvantages as well as advantages.

Group decision making The literature abounds with descriptions of how individuals and groups differ in decision making effectiveness. The consensus seems to be that groups are more likely to incorporate a diversity of backgrounds and perspectives, which provides a full airing of issues. Many heads are, indeed, often better than one, because greater knowledge and information will generate more potential solutions that will receive general support than any one individual's program. Often, the greatest benefit of strategic planning is that it fosters discussion of vital issues that might not otherwise have taken place.

On the other hand, the safety assured from the greater number of participants in the decision making process can give way to a presumption of invulnerability, a short step from decision making arrogance and recklessness. Groups involved in the strategic planning process need to be aware of the available data and the group's accumulated knowledge for scanning the environment, as well as the need for continued, conscious scrutiny of the resulting goals, objectives, and strategies.

In the context of strategic planning, group decision making appears most useful when issues are new or complex and require a broader range of problem-solving approaches, when it is possible to build consensus, and when it is necessary to counter minor opposition through the involvement of more individuals or groups.

The group approach to strategic decision making may be of less value when the group does not have adequate authority or when its conclusions are regularly vetoed by the chief administrator or others outside the group. Similarly, if individuals in the group do not enjoy their involvement in the strategic planning of the association's future, the group approach may be ill-advised.

In addition to the dynamics of group decision making, the actual mechanics are important as well. Groups can become cumbersome and produce written products more slowly in direct proportion to the number of individuals involved.

Some basic rules of group involvement in the strategic planning process include the following:

1. Ensure that the group is large enough to incorporate a wide range of perspectives but small enough that it does not become unwieldy
2. Ensure that the support of top management for both the group and the process is clear to all who are directly involved
3. Make available to the group the resources and status necessary to carry out the function of strategic planning, including access to data and people
4. Include the senior executive, the chairman, or some other key individual in the planning process and encourage this person to check with the group on a regular basis
5. Encourage the development of new ideas and programs and creative approaches to existing programs

If the group begins on this basis, it will enjoy the freedom, support, and flexibility to be creative in its planning and resolute in its recommendations.

Finally, the group must be dedicated not only to the premise that strategic planning is a useful tool, but also to the notion that it is a process that will require single-minded devotion. Strategic planning groups often become institutionalized for the purpose of ongoing review and planning for subsequent cycles. Even the task of planning for a single cycle can take a major expenditure of time. And, like many endeavors, the time tends to increase in direct proportion to the number of participants and contested issues involved, and to decrease in proportion to the number of times the planning process has been previously employed by the organization.

Ethics and strategic planning

Sensitivity to ethics is important in strategic planning. Exceptional opportunities must be reviewed, but their consideration must be tempered by acceptable standards of individual conduct. When appropriate, planners may even incorporate into the final document objectives and strategies that encourage ethical behavior on the part of those implementing the plan.

Association executives must be ever mindful of the ethical implications of either the fact or the appearance of using organizational funds or resources to benefit themselves or special interests, rather than the membership at large. This includes accepting gifts or favors from those with whom professional interaction might occur, giving preference to associates in treatment or in the provision of member services, conducting outside financial dealings, and receiving honoraria or external employment.

Issues of ethical behavior turn not solely on facts; the appearance of propriety plays an equally vital role. Supreme Court Justice Louis Brandeis once wrote, "Honesty by itself is not enough. The appearance of integrity must be concomitant."

Ethical considerations can arise at any point in the strategic planning process. Those who regard and analyze the environment need to remain impartial to their own background, constituency, program area, and personal agenda if the environmental scan is to represent the best view of the future. Clearly, it would be unethical to mask a problem or to highlight an issue artificially through the analytical process.

The projection of revenues, costs, and fiscal obligations of an association must be performed with accuracy and concern for what is best for the membership. If such forecasts are inflated or deflated, the results can be either the unnecessary deletion of program opportunities from the goals, objectives, and strategies, or the inclusion of allocations for which resources will not exist.

While a certain amount of uncertainty in those forecasts will always exist, spending questions can be resolved either by taking a very conservative position or by funding programs in priority order. The latter permits the funding of the critical or desirable programs initially, with additional operations or levels of operations receiving funds as actual revenue levels become more clear. What must be avoided is controlling program approval through the restriction or inflation of resource projections.

The key principle that must guide the process is that the environmental scan is a factual exercise. It must provide the most accurate scenarios possible so the decision makers can render their judgments about general directions, programs, and resource allocations on the basis of the most accurate and comprehensive information.

The appearance of ethical standards of behavior is critical to the ultimate acceptability of the plan. A few general guidelines can help ensure both the ethics and the perception of ethical behavior throughout the process.

First, if there is a need because of competition for funds to protect the confidentiality of some information, this should be stated up front, with an explanation of what will be protected, why, and how.

Second, it may be useful to review with those involved in the planning process the relevant standards of conduct in the charter, and the codes of professional organizations such as ASAE. It may even be useful to incorporate such written standards into the inherent beliefs section of the written plan.

A third means of ensuring the perception of ethical procedures is to provide total access to members throughout the process. This can be accomplished by including in the committee deliberations or members who are well-respected in the association, persons of different professional areas, and persons representing a diversity of backgrounds and beliefs.

It is for these reasons that many associations actually list their codes of ethics in the final strategic planning document. The following code of ethics is extracted from the plan of the International Facilities Management Association:

1. IFMA members shall have as their primary goal developing and managing safe, humane, and functional work environments
2. IFMA members shall integrate the needs of management with the needs of people in the workplace to develop and manage humane and effective work environments
3. IFMA members shall have as an achievable goal maintaining objective, professional judgment. They shall not compromise that judgment by undertaking any activity, accepting any contribution, or having any conflict of interest that would prevent acting in the best interest of their employees, clients, or those people for whom they provide or maintain workplaces
4. IFMA members shall practice in a manner that supports the rights of employers, employees, and clients, and shall not discriminate because of race, sex, creed, age, or national origin
5. IFMA members shall continually seek new information to maintain their skills relative to the design, construction, maintenance, and management of the physical environment as it relates to people and work processes
6. IFMA members shall use IFMA membership solely as a means of professional development, not for purposes of selling or personal aggrandizement

The Role of Human Resources Management

Strategic planning as a process will take different forms in different settings. Variations on the theme may result from factors already noted, including organizational maturity, the stage of evolution of the planning process itself, and the inherent beliefs and personalities of the elected officers and the senior management of the association. As has been discussed, the flow of the process can also vary from one organization to the next. And, of course, different organizations will involve different individuals in the process.

Often, the group's human resources manager is not so directly involved in developing the plan as in its later implementation. However, when one considers the potential impact of revisions to established programs and ways of doing things, and of entirely new endeavors, the effects of strategic planning on the organization's human resources become evident. Although senior managers and supervisors share the responsibility for human resources planning and development, much of the work falls on the human resources manager. The value of the human resources manager in the planning process itself becomes clear.

The functions of such managers normally include: recruitment and selection; internal personnel movement (promotions, demotions, dismissals, and succession planning); organizational development; training and professional development; wage and benefits issues; job descriptions, performance standards, and performance appraisals; and record-keeping. Every one of these areas may be affected by the association's strategic plan. Thus, it is good to include the managers of these functions in the planning process.

As each of these areas is potentially affected by strategic planning, so each of these areas can contribute to the process of encouraging strategic thinking. Here the human resources manager can play several roles. Figure 5.1 illustrates these roles for each phase in the strategic planning process. At the left are the elements in the strategic plan and at the top are the human resources functions.

Each cell in the matrix reflects the potential roles for the human resources manager. The code *a* represents data analysis and forecasting: *c*, communications; *d*, decision making; and *g*, providing guidance. As one might expect, there are some cells for which a logical role either does not exist or is minimal. These areas are represented in the matrix by *n/a* (not applicable).

For example, the mission statement reflects the essential reason for the existence of the organization. One of the greatest services the human resources manager can perform for an organization is to ensure that all employees fully understand the mission and incorporate it into their daily activities. It should be reflected in the organization's structure and be communicated to those who make decisions about promotions and succession into key positions. It should serve as the basis for orienting new staff and developing existing personnel. And because it portrays the very essence of the organization, it should be an integral part of an individual's performance standards and annual appraisals. The human resources manager's role with respect to the mission statement is, first and foremost, one of communication, represented by the letter *c* in the figure.

Other roles in relation to the mission statement involve its incorporation into decisions about the growth and structure of the organization. As an organization grows, its structure, reporting relationships, and culture can change. They evolve either within the confines of the existing organization or as the result of a conscious decision. There is a role here for the human resources manager to provide input into decisions affecting structural changes in the organization and the preparation of individuals to fit into new areas in support of such changes.

The internal and external environmental scans identify the myriad of factors which affect the ability of the organization to achieve its goals continued on page 102

Figure 5.1. The strategic planning/human resources matrix

	Recruitment/ Selection	Internal Personnel Movement	Organizational Development	Training and Development	Wage Benefits	Job Descrip-tion	Record Keeping
Mission Statement	c	cdg	cdg	cdg	n/a	c	n/a
Beliefs	c	cd	n/a	cdg	n/a	cg	n/a
Environmental Scans	adg	adg	acg	ag	ag	acg	ag
Goals and Objectives	ag	acg	cg	acg	a	acg	a
Strategies and Implementation Plans	acd	acdg	cg	cdg	ag	ac	a
Contingency Planning	n/a	g	acg	cg	acd	n/a	acg
Controls and Feedback	adg	ag	ag	ag	ag	ag	ag

Role codes: a= Data analysis and forecasting; c= Communications; n/a= Not applicable; d= Decision making; d= Providing Guidance and objectives. The internal scan gives the human resources manager the opportunity to identify strengths and weaknesses in existing personnel, to project needs for new or different staff or skills, and to develop programs to upgrade existing personnel.

Perhaps the most critical role will be to analyze staff capabilities and match them against future needs to prepare for, and to help assess the costs of, the new plans.

Whether the new goals and objectives can be accomplished through the retraining or redeployment of existing staff and resources or through the acquisition of new, the impact will be felt in terms of recruitment, internal personnel shifts, training and professional development programs, wage and benefits decisions, and job analyses and performance standards. The role of the human resources manager here is to analyze the gaps between current capabilities and projected needs, to decide what actions should be taken to prepare for the new directions of the association, and to communicate this information to the appropriate persons.

The strategies and implementation plans extend the process one step further, to the level of individual performance: that is, who will do what? To the extent that an organization's top management feels comfortable in disseminating such information, this can be vital to the success of the plan. It is at this stage that the plan becomes real to most employees. This is what they will do on a day-to-day basis; the goals and objectives illustrate why.

In this critical phase, the human resources manager must ensure that the "what" and the "why" of the plans are communicated in a clear and consistent manner. It is rarely enough to simply explain what is in the plan for the individual and the organization when the plan is new; it must be continually reinforced to ensure ongoing understanding, cooperation, and support.

For the human resources manager, there will be considerations beyond the communication of intent and the impact of the plan. There will also be a need to analyze the efficiency of new operations and persons involved in them, to determine the need for recruitment of new personnel or redeployment of existing personnel. Similarly, organizational shifts to support new programs may be detrimental to ongoing operations. These impacts – on the association as a whole, and on the individual – must be assessed and communicated, along with appropriate recommendations, to senior management.

Controls and feedback are mechanisms designed to gauge the progress being made toward the plan's objectives, to isolate areas requiring fine-tuning, and to ensure that the lessons of operating in one planning cycle are regularly and formally incorporated into subsequent plans. The human resources manager is in an ideal situation to contribute relevant data to support these efforts. Where this is the case, he or she should assemble and analyze the data and make appropriate follow-up recommendations.

Thus, the role of the human resources manager is vital not only to the implementation of an organization's plan but also to its preparation. Organizations are comprised of individuals and, like individuals, each operates in its own distinctive style. In some, the human resources managers may already be involved in strategic planning. In others, this person may not have such a role. To the extent that the human resources manager has a distinct perspective on the organization and its employees, it is critical to reflect that knowledge in the preparation, implementation, and revision of strategic plans. The result will be felt in terms of: the stability and productivity of employees; the greater acceptance of, and response to, the plan; the provision and preparation of required personnel; and the assessment and improvement of overall performance.

Chapter 6

The Role of Forecasting

In strategic planning, alternative future scenarios are identified to highlight the problems and opportunities associated with each and to enable decision makers to select the goals, objectives, and strategies that are most likely to direct the association toward the desired vision of the future. Forecasting helps decision makers understand better the various scenarios. Sound forecasts may lend credibility to some alternatives and discredit others.

The process of formal strategic planning has emerged relatively recently, and forecasting is an even more recent addition to the process. However, forecasting has always taken place in professional organizations, although the methods may have been rudimentary or intuitive.

What has emerged in recent years is a conscious effort to incorporate forecasting methods into the strategic planning process and to increase the sophistication and accuracy of forecasting. This has led to a reexamination and wider acceptance of the methods involved.

Once forecasting was accepted as an integral part of

the strategic planning process, the methods in use came under scrutiny. Older methods tended to be most accurate when a high degree of constancy existed in the historical data. Trends, cycles, or seasonal adjustments which had recurred over time were expected to be seen again in the future.

The Nature of Forecasting

All methods of forecasting are designed to predict what will happen in the future on the basis of past performance. Some such projections are relatively easy and entail less uncertainty than others. The difference results from the amount or complexity of the data, the distance in time of the future scenario, or the number of variables which must interact to produce the projected result: the forecast.

Every forecasting technique, however, has some common elements. Although each attempts to predict a future situation, none can do so with absolute accuracy. Forecasts, regardless of the behavior of the past data, are depictions of future activity and future data interrelationships. Sophistication of technique and experience aside, the future remains an unknown. The best forecasters can do is to continue to improve the practice and to develop and hone new techniques.

The selection of a forecasting method depends on the amount, accessibility, and reliability of historical data. Obviously, as more reliable data are available to build a historical pattern, the better will be the resulting projections. The selection of a method also depends on the level of detail desired. As the decisions involved require greater levels of detail in the forecast, the choice of techniques to use becomes more complex. There is a paradox in the relationship between the number of data elements involved in the forecast and the complexity of the technique involved. At some point, the sheer volume of data requires that the technique used be simpler. With fewer historical data points and fewer factors involved, the forecaster can often afford to apply more complex techniques.

Categories of forecasting

Two broad categories of forecasting exist: judgmental methods and quantitative methods. Judgmental methods rely on the collective, intuitive wisdom of those involved. Prior to the emergence of strategic planning and forecasting as professional endeavors, personal judgment was often all that was available to decision makers to decide where their organizations should turn next.

Quantitative methods don't guarantee either the accuracy of the forecast or the sensibility of the plan. But they do provide additional data bearing on the future and increase the chances that the forecast will be realistic.

There are two types of quantitative methods. Time series methods assume that consistent, recurrent patterns in the data can be expected to occur again and again. They assume that these trends, cycles, and seasonal variations will not be significantly affected in the future by changes in the environmental conditions that have historically shaped them. Causal methods, on the other hand, assume that changes in the environment will have predictable effects on dependent variables in the future. They assume that environmental factors and relationships change over time and that past patterns may not recur.

Precautions in the use of forecasts

The user of forecasts must be constantly aware of many potential pitfalls. First, the accuracy of any projection into the future necessarily rests on the accuracy of assumptions made about what data to include in that forecast and how much weight to give it. Again, the milieu of any forecast is the future, so one can never be certain.

Second, forecasters have a tendency to limit the acceptance of their own projections. Due to the inherent uncertainty of forecasts and the human desire not to be wrong, projections are often heavily laden with conditions and assumptions. Forecasts that hedge the bets too much lose much of their value.

A final note

Studies of forecasting techniques indicate that one method is selected over another on the basis of several factors. These include the ease of application and comprehension, the credibility of the technique in previous applications, the flexibility of the model to changing input, and the associated costs.

Regardless of the model or technique chosen, it is critical to remember that all of the possible selections require human decisions. The relative value of the input is determined by humans. The meaning of the output must be determined by humans. Forecasting is an art as much as a science, and as a science it is inexact. While it helps strategic planners understand various future scenarios better, it is not a guarantee. It simply improves the odds.

Chapter 7

Summary and Conclusions

The basis of this book is that the process of strategic planning is largely the same for an association as in a private, for-profit business. It requires similar support among the organizations management to be effective; it requires internal communication to support the concept and contents; and it requires a thorough understanding of the past, present, and future environments in which the organization must function in developing goals, objectives, and strategies. In neither milieu is planning a guarantee of either success or the absence of failure.

While the process is the same in the association and the private sectors, there are some differences. The stakeholders in an association may have a more direct interest in the successful operation of the organization. For them, it is not a matter simply of brand loyalty which can be switched should the preferred product line be discontinued. For many association members, the very existence of their businesses may be at stake, or progress toward an important medical solution or social situation. In such cases, stakeholders will be more involved, more vocal, perhaps even more cautious.

In spite of these many, substantial differences, the order of the process remains remarkably similar in the association and the private sectors. The benefits of planning and the disadvantages of not planning are also similar. The relative size of the membership for which the strategic plan is being developed has little or no bearing on the order or structure of the process. The order of the process and of the ultimate product, the written plan, should be similar for all organizations. And, of course, the direct relationship of the plan's goals, objectives, and strategies to the allocation of scarce resources is a constant from one plan to the next, regardless of the size of the association for which it was developed.

Resources for strategic planning

An association need not advance through the strategic planning process as if it was the first association to do so. Assistance is available from a variety of sources, including the American Planning Association, the American Management Association, and others. There are many statewide and regional counterparts to these associations which can provide direction, support, and data.

Organizations which represent associations, such as the ASAE or local societies, can also provide relevant resource materials.

Frequently, the strategic planning process can be improved by the use of a process facilitator or a consultant who is sufficiently outside the organization to envision new approaches without being hampered by preconceived notions. Often, a person exists locally who has a basic understanding of association issues and resources without being steeped in history or process. Or there may be someone with this insight who has retained sufficient distance to remain unbiased to the future and its potential.

It might even be possible for an association to "borrow" a strategic planner from a similar organization. This would permit the exchange of ideas with someone who has experience with the process in a similar setting.

Finally, one must not overlook the private sector. Local businesses may have a long-term investment in the strategic planning process and, as corporate citizens, may be willing to share their expertise. The private sector is generally adept at problem-solving, financial and asset management, and opportunity identification.

In short, resources abound. Prudent decision makers will take advantage of and mold them to fit and facilitate the local process.

Innovation in association management

One of the primary benefits of strategic planning is that it permits and encourages the emergence of innovative approaches and programs. There is a popular misconception that innovation is the domain of for-profit business, that monetary profit is the bottom line which provides the incentive to do new things or to do the same things in better, more imaginative ways. Innovation, however, can exist in any environment. The bottom line to which businesses refer is simply one motivator of new ideas.

An association also has a bottom line: the revenue side of the budget. As dues and fees decline or the demand for more or better member services increases, the non-business bottom line constricts. Often an association has decreasing revenues at the same time it must increase its levels of service. Then a need arises for newer or better ways of doing things. This need drives innovative thinking — the introduction of new ideas or methods, or new ways of approaching old problems.

In the strategic plan, it is important to encourage innovation in addressing the problems and opportunities identified in the environmental scan. The objectives and strategies are areas in which innovative methods can be developed. Association planners and senior staff and leadership should ensure that an environment is provided in which innovative ideas are not just permitted, but encouraged and nurtured.

Planning to plan

One must plan to plan. This is true whether an association is doing a plan for the first time or the fifty-first. It is as true in associations as in the business world. The stakeholders may be more numerous and may have greater access to the process, and scans may need to touch upon different factors, but the process is the same for an association as for a business.

Strategic plans frequently acknowledge the ongoing nature of the process. Including a formal statement in the plan itself will provide a constant reminder of the need to reconvene, review and replan. Such statements may be brief reminders that review and replanning will take place. Others may be more specific as to the timing and ongoing responsibilities of the planning committee. A good example, a statement from the plan of the Washington, D.C.-based American Pharmaceutical Association, is provided for the reader's information in Appendix XI.

Strategic planning can spell the difference between success and failure for an organization. It can encourage employees at all levels to stretch to achieve a higher plane of thought and performance. It can result in the optimal allocation of scarce budgetary resources. It can give employees and members a greater sense of their stake in the organization and a better feeling about its future and their own.

Chapter 8

Strategic Planning: A Step-by-Step Guide

Following is an outline of steps in the process and product of strategic planning:

I. Identify the need for strategic planning
  A. Explain the benefits of the strategic planning process
  B. Explain the strategic planning process
  C. Solicit support for the strategic planning process from:
    1. Elected boards and officers
    2. Senior managers
    3. Department heads and key staff
    4. Members

II. Announce the decision to use the process and the expected benefits to:
  A. Employees
  B. Key members of the board, committee, etc.
  C. Members

III. Determine the structure of the process
   A. Decision-making approach (top-down, bottom-up, or combination)
   B. Review process
   C. Approval process
   D. Schedule

IV. Select the participants
   A. Elected leadership
   B. Senior managers
   C. Employees
   D. Relevant regulatory bodies
   E. External representatives
      1. Board and committee members
      2. Other relevant service providers
      3. Interest groups

V. Impanel the group
   A. Convene the first meeting
   B. Announce, appoint, or select a chairman
   C. Issue the charge to the group
   D. Review the schedule
      1. Meetings
      2. Products
      3. First draft
      4. Final draft
      5. Reporting requirements and the review process
      6. Approval process
      7. Timing of the implementation
   E. Announce support and incentives for the planning group
      1. Rewards of success
      2. Support of the local leadership
      3. Guidance available
   F. Develop committee structure, membership, and operating principles

VI. Lay the groundwork
   A. Identify the mission from the charter, state law, or other source
   B. Develop a mission statement if none exists
   C. Through interviews and other means, identify key decision makers and their inherent beliefs

VII. Conduct the environmental scan
   A. Structure the scanning matrix
      1. Identify the environments to be scanned
      2. Identify the environmental factors to be observed in each environment
   B. Using the environmental scanning matrix (Figure 2.2), assign the review process for each cell (each factor within each environment) to a person or persons
   C. Ensure that participants develop a full understanding of each cell
   D. Reconvene the planning group or assemble the intelligence it has gathered
   E. Describe the possible scenarios for the future
   F. Detail the single description which most accurately depicts the future
   G. Ensure that participants discuss the description of the future for concurrence and understanding
   H. Review the scenario of the future and extract from it:
      1. Internal weaknesses
      2. Internal strengths
      3. External opportunities
      4. External threats

VIII. Review the scan and its conclusions
   A. Achieve the maximum consensus on goals
   B. Develop objectives for each goal
   C. Achieve the maximum consensus on objectives
   D. Develop strategies for each objective

E. Achieve the maximum consensus on strategies
F. Develop initial implementation plans
G. Develop as many contingency situations as possible
H. Develop plans for each contingency situation
I. Develop control mechanisms and incorporate into the plan

IX. Prepare a written plan
A. Assign writers to prepare a draft
B. Review draft internally
C. Revise draft as needed
D. Submit revised draft for external review to elected officials, civic groups, and other stakeholders
E. Revise draft again as needed

X. Submit the plan to the governing body for official adoption

XI. Publicize the plan to:
A. Members
B. Trade media
C. Others

XII. Implement the plan
A. Implement strategies
B. Design and institute controls
C. Monitor and assess ongoing performance
D. Assess feedback and revise implementation plans as needs

XIII. Prepare for next planning cycle
A. Ensure that feedback is captured for future planning cycles
B. Outline and schedule next planning cycle

Appendix I

Inherent Beliefs

The Music Educators National Conference:

1. Music education is a lifetime process that involves teachers at all levels and learners of all ages and special needs.

2. The musical heritage of America's people is threatened in today's changing society.

3. The importance of music in American society and in the education of children requires a strong advocacy program for music in education.

4. Music is a dynamic, creative art in which innovations and changes will occur.

5. The continuing existence and nature of music education will be determined, in part, by the desire and ability of music educators to identify new relationships, change attitudes, and define innovative objectives and processes.

6. Policies at all levels of government can affect music education.

7. Voluntary national standards in music if adopted and implemented at state

and local levels can significantly improve music education in the U.S. for all children.

8. Funding is inadequate for education in general, and for music education in particular.

9. Many individuals who impact education have neither the knowledge nor the experience to make informed decisions about music education.

10. Social issues and changing demographic patterns present new and significant challenges for music educators (e.g., increased diversity, changing values, substance abuse, changes in family structure, and violence in society).

11. Gender, ethnicity, special needs, economic status, and geographic location may affect access to music education.

12. Education reform initiatives influence changes in music education (e.g., national standards, assessment, alternative schooling, scheduling, site-based management, integrated curriculum, graduation requirements, and pre- and in-service teacher training).

13. The shift of decision making power from traditional educational leadership to business, industry, national policy making agencies, and local educational sites affects music education.

14. Changes in state certification/licensure requirements, alternative certification/licensure, and use of non-certified/non-licensed personnel impact the delivery and quality of music education.

15. Requirements in teacher education curricula, as developed by schools of education and accredited agencies, impact music teacher education.

16. Changes in technology impact music education at all levels.

The Door and Hardware Institute:

1. Our members are the focus of everything we do. Members are our owners. Our work must be done with them in mind, providing the best possible products and services.

2. Quality comes first. To achieve member satisfaction, the quality of our products and services in meeting current and future member needs must be our top priority.

3. Continuous improvement is essential to our success. We recognize that excellence, once achieved, must be maintained and improved, and that we must all work together constantly to upgrade our products and services to meet member needs.

4. Teamwork is our way of life. Members and staff treat each other with trust and respect, recognizing that the role of members is to develop strategy and policy with staff assistance, and the role of staff is to carry out the strategies and policies with member assistance.

5. Financial responsibility guides our decision making. When developing programs, products, and services, we think through the immediate and long-term financial implications of our actions, and make prudent funding provisions in advance to support them throughout their lifespan.

6. DHI is committed to diversity. In principle and practice, we foster a diverse membership and promote full participation in the programs and decision making bodies of the organization.

7. Our integrity is never compromised. DHI operates in a professional and responsible manner that commands respect for its integrity and for its positive contributions to society.

8. We are leaders, not followers. We work to create our own future through the practice of strategic management principles.

9. We seek mutually beneficial relationships with constituents. DHI and its members can only prosper if we have positive interaction with a wide variety of outside interests.

Appendix II

Typical Factors for the Environmental Scan

The American Association of School Administrators

Category: Economic

Factors	Predictions	Impact
1. Public School Revenue	A. general fund revenue mandated by formula from state	A.1. limits programs 2. limits staff 3. limits supplies/ materials 4. affects class size 5. possible school closures 6. reduction of building maintenance
	B. board choice to hold budget/bond election	B.1. revenues not guaranteed 2. polarizes community

Category: Demographic

Factors	Predictions	Impact
1. Median Age	A. percent of population over age 65 will increase	A.1. increase in demand for social service 2. increase in competition for tax dollars 3. increase in taxpayer resistance to tax increases for education 4. diminishment of support 5. availability of senior citizens to community 6. increase in number of potential volunteers 7. significant number of staff retirements 8. replacement of staff increasingly difficult 9. increase in demand for adult education 10. increased use of facilities 11. potential for increase in alienation between direct consumers of education and the elderly 12. more demand for food programs

Source: William J. Cook, Jr., Ph.D. *Strategic Planning for America's Schools*. Arlington, Virginia: American Association of School Administrators, 1995, pp. 58-59.

Appendix III

The Environmental Scan: A Description of Conclusions

The American Association of Law Libraries

Prelude: The 1990's are a time of change. Changes in technology, in the means of publication, in the economy, and in libraries of all types, are causing fundamental shifts in the ways in which legal information is produced and disseminated, along with the ways in which we deliver that information to our clients. Moreover, changes in the Association have made it larger, more dynamic, more diverse, and more complex than ever before.

External Environment

Technology, Changing Roles, and Professional Education

Without any doubt, the greatest concern expressed by the members of AALL in the various surveys and focus groups leading up to this plan, was the impact of technology on libraries in general and their own law library in particular. As recently as the early 1970's, most law libraries were paper collections of primary legal materials, one, or at most two, journals from each law school, and a manageable number of treatises on an array of legal topics. To this print collection was quickly added a variety of microform materials and two small but growing legal data bases, Lexis and Westlaw. More recently, it has seemed that every major publisher has turned to cd-rom as another means to disseminate its products. At the same time more new data bases have become necessary to meet the needs of our clients: Legislate, Dialog, CQ, Dow-Jones, and a number of others.

On top of this already complex world of information is the bewildering array of legal information just beginning to emerge on the Internet. It seems that almost every source of primary legal information is making or planning to make that information available via the 'Net. In many ways, these sources simply replace what was previously available in other forms. For example, many courts are now disseminating (but not necessarily retaining) their own (slip) opinions electronically. In other cases, these new data bases will make readily available what was previously difficult to locate, such as information on the current bills in the various state legislatures. The information that is available in these new forms changes daily as new databases are announced, Internet addresses are changed, and new delivery systems (WAIS, Gopher, World Wide Web, Mosaic) are developed and released.

As so many new ways of acquiring legal information are developed and announced, the situation resembles nothing so much as the Lexis starfield screen with more and more stars rushing toward us at an ever-increasing speed. As law librarians, we have access to more information in a greater diversity of formats than ever before. At the same time, much of the information has no bibliographic control, is in non-standardized formats, has no convenient mechanism for searching, and is not in a form likely to be preserved for future researchers. These difficulties of using and making available the newest forms of information are issues that are likely to challenge the profession for some years to come.

Despite the problems, the new systems are fundamentally changing the profession. Some even suggested that the newest of the trends foreshadow some significant downsizing, or even the elimination of libraries as physical spaces in certain circumstances. Even if such a development occurs, it does not and should not necessarily mean the elimination of the legal information professional. But, different skills will be needed for the legal information manager at the turn of the century than was true even just a few years ago. Not only must we be familiar with "Statutes at Large," "Federal Cases," and "Corbin on Contracts," we must also know how to navigate the Internet. We are more likely to be talking today about Gopher, Telnet, and FTP than about Blackstone and Coke.

All of this signals a shift in the role of the librarian, almost a change in the definition of the term. As the information officers for our law firm, law school, or other legal organization, our task is now to manage a vast , and largely uncharted sea of information, to map out the islands of legal information, and to make them readily accessible to our clients.

As our role changes, the nature of our professional education will also change. But as a significant number of library schools have closed over the last few years, the challenge to rethink the requirements for entry into the profession will increasingly fall to the profession itself. Indeed, it may be that if library schools continue to close, the professional associations will have to fill the void.

Such profound changes are as unsettling to many of those with whom we have worked in the past as they are to us. Publishers are uncertain about their future, and even within our own parent organizations, turf issues are arising between the librarians as information professionals and the technical people who provide computer support and administer the local networks. Whatever tensions may exist, it is clear that in the end we will need to work together in the best interests of legal researchers, the lawyers, judges, and law students and faculty, who are our clients.

The Economy

Most of the 1980s were growth years. Law firms expanded. Starting salaries for lawyers and applications for law school reached all-time highs. Libraries of all sizes and types automated their operations, and the personal computer, which began in a garage in the late 1970s, was ubiquitous by the end of the '80s.

By the late '80s and early '90s, however, the rapid growth had come to an end. Federal, state, and local budgets were under severe pressure, and publicly supported libraries of all types faced cuts in hours and programs as well as cuts to the materials budgets. Law school budgets were often stagnant, and some academic law libraries saw cuts to the book budget and staff that were unthinkable a few years before. Even law firms were not immune to the recession. Law firms that expanded only a few years before being laying off lawyers, and clients began questioning the Lexis and Westlaw fees added on to their bill. Every part of the operation, including the library was subject to greater scrutiny concerning their costs and their contribution to the bottom line.

In the middle 1990s, the recession has largely come to an end, but the rapid growth has not returned and no one seems to be predicting that it will. Law firms are making fewer permanent hires, law school library budgets are barely keeping up with inflation, and many governments are still trying to find ways to downsize.

During this same period, there has been an increasing concentration among traditional legal publishers. Shephards, for example, was purchased by McGraw Hill. Many of the new owners of American legal publishers are outside the United States. Thomson and Thomson (a Canadian company) purchased a number of legal publishers including Callahan, Clark-Boardman, Warren Gorham & Lamont, R.I.A., Lawyer's Coop., Sweet & Maxwell, Carswell, and several others. PrenticeHall was purchased by Maxwell-MacMillan which in turn sold it to Thomson who divided the publications among their different divisions. UPA and CIS are both owned by Elsevier, a Dutch company. In turn, Elsevier was purchased by Reed, which is based in London. Even as the concentration increased among the traditional publishers some new publishers have emerged to provide access to legal information in electronic form. Counterpoint is providing access to the "Federal Register" on the Internet, and several start-up companies are developing new techniques to provide legal information on cd-rom.

AALL has held its own during the recession, but members have shown an increased desire to understand the value they receive for the money they put into the association. Even the "Biographical Directory" and the "Law Library Journal" have been questioned. Attendance at the annual meeting has remained basically stable and even increased somewhat, as the attendance at the 1993 annual meeting in Boston was the highest ever. However, in the same year, two pre-conference institutes had to be canceled because of insufficient enrollment. Some felt that fewer members were able to take the extra time necessary to attend an institute in addition to the annual meeting. Educational programs are in high demand, but the association needs to take care that they are affordable and that, whenever possible, they are available in a variety of locations to minimize the need to travel. Similarly, as the economy has put more pressure on law film librarians, it appears that fewer of them will be able to find the time to volunteer on behalf of the Association.

Public Policy Environment

AALL has been involved in Public Information Policy since about 1989. Then, many of the issues centered on the efforts of the Reagan and Bush administrations to reduce access to federal government information in a variety of ways. In general, the effort was either to privatize the function directly as when the Reagan administration proposed to privatize the NTIS, or to do it indirectly by reducing government output and creating a climate conducive to business with policies that favored private dissemination over government dissemination. Throughout the period, specific publications were eliminated, funding for the government depository program remained flat, and many proposals were made (and mostly fended off) to keep the government out of publishing. (It was said, for example, that the government should not compete with the private sector; indeed, it was said that the government should not even develop an information product if private sector companies "might" be developing a similar product).

With the change of administrations, the issues have shifted rather dramatically. The Clinton administration has not rolled back the Reagan-Bush policies; rather, they have struck out in an entirely new direction. The government is no longer trying affirmatively to reduce dissemination; instead, the Clinton-Gore administration has proposed the development of a National Information Infrastructure for the exchange of all kinds of electronic information nationwide. Dissemination of government information over the NII is a key component of the administration proposal, and many agencies are anticipating an electronic future by developing methods and systems for the announcement of rules and decisions, and the release of other information products electronically.

As a result of the Clinton-Gore proposal, the issues are now quite different than under the previous administration. Telecommunications regulation and the structuring of a communications environment that will promote appropriate policy goals are now the focus. Among these are the need for "universal access," protection of individual privacy, open access for a variety of information providers, encryption of information and access to systems by law enforcement agencies, etc. In addition, of course, it is necessary to ensure that government agencies do, in fact, have the right and obligation to disseminate their information electronically without undue costs or restrictions on users. Further some vigilance will be needed to ensure that the public continues to enjoy a right of free access to federal government information as they have under the Depository Library Program.

Copyright has also emerged as a major issue for the first time since the passage of the Copyright Reform Act in 1976. Finding appropriate ways to protect the interests of copyright owners when their works are disseminated over the National Information Infrastructure is deemed one of the keys to the success of the NII. At the same time, the library community is concerned to protect some semblance of fair use and the rights they have enjoyed under the 1976 Act for interlibrary and preservation. Fair use promotes the use of materials for purposes of research and scholarship. Preservation may be even more important in the electronic environment than for paper, since works disseminated electronically are, by their nature, volatile and probably short-lived. Someone will need to take steps in a coordinated and systematic way to preserve such materials or they will inevitably be lost to history. The resolution of these complex issues is fundamental for the eventual success of the National Information Infrastructure as a medium of dissemination.

Appendix IV

The Environmental Scan Summarized

The Printing Industries of America, Inc.

Impacts From Core Issues

WHAT'S HAPPENING	CONSEQUENCES
Technology:	
Technological innovations are causing significant reduction in barriers to changing printing processes	The industry will continue to expand and be entrepreneurial at the "low end" even as merger and acquisition creates more con centration at the high end.
	Electronic printing including variable imaging will grow as a competitive

The composition of the information industry is changing. Print's share of the information pie is declining. However, the absolute size of the pie is growing rapidly which means that printer's absolute volume (including ancillary services) continues to grow.	medium to offset print ing.
	Members must think of their business in new ways if they are to establish themselves in new roles as gate-keepers on the digital information highway.
New sources of value are created as the information process restructures.	PIA must identify the new and emerging value-added opportunities in non-traditional printing, ancillary services, and alternative media.
	A changing perspective on members — who they are, membership requirements, national versus local, etc.
	Provide members additional information on technology alternatives and printers' use of technology.

Customer Relationships:

Customer expectations are changing greatly.	Value-added moves downstream as printers become integrators reproducing data in many forms.
	The industry is changing from manufacturing to service, from a

	"back office" or downstream sector to a "customer-oriented" or upstream function.
Capital Investment:	
Investment needed per unit of quality output is declining.	Industry financing needs are changing from long-term purchase of "iron" to short-term ongoing financing of digital equipment.
Human Resources:	
Industry jobs are becoming deskilled and knowledge is more portable to and from other industries.	A change in the education focus, and a need for new knowledge and skills, courses, and seminars
Markets:	
Changes in the composition of certain market segments will bring about new competition between "local" printers and "national" printers. Large and small printers may find themselves competing against each other more often.	PIA should investigate ways for local printers to network to provide a "publish centrally, print locally" option for members This should include investigation of a gate way for networks such as the Internet.

Appendix V

The SWOT Analysis: Strengths, Weaknesses, Opportunities, and Threats

The International Association of Financial Planning

Strengths:

Our members help consumers achieve financial independence, which is a worthy objective, on whose behalf we are proud to work.

Our scope is industry-wide, encompassing all financial advisers (regardless of their background or designation), broker-dealers, and companies who sell products and services to or through financial advisers; we are the only open forum organization.

IAFP is the oldest (founded in 1969) and largest leading financial planning association, and has helped develop financial planning as a profession.

We have developed a majestic, long-term vision, mission, passion, and franchise for IAFP, with input from many members.

Membership is growing again.

IAFP is well known and respected by those in the regulatory and legislative arena.

The association has long-standing and generally cordial relationships with both consumer and trade media.

We offer a broad-based education and training program, with programs for beginners and advanced planners, specialists and generalists, those who are technically oriented and those who are marketing oriented.

The IAFP Consumer Referral Program is a mechanism for consumers to identify qualified financial planning practitioners.

Included in our membership are the leaders in our industry.

The Association has financial reserves equal to one year's annual operating expenses.

Local and national leadership is dedicated and hard working.

We have a strong, effective ethics program.

Our 110 chapters provide local education and networking opportunities for most members.

The national Board has committed to focus its time on strategic direction, and leave operations to the staff.

We have an experienced staff and effective staff leadership focusing on responding to the Board's strategic direction.

Members have increasing opportunities to become involved at the national level through our councils and task forces.

New member benefits introduced in the past several years have enhanced the perception of value of national membership.

IAFP membership provides excellent value for the dues.

Weaknesses:

Some parts of what we say, promote, or stand for conflict with others.

Our industry-wide membership makes it hard to reach consensus on some issues and can diffuse our focus.

There has been a perception of lack of value of the national association to both individuals and chapters.

The relationship between IAFP and its chapters has improved but it can still at times be less than fulfilling to one or both parties.

The magazine, perceived as a primary benefit, is not owned or controlled by the Association.

Few members are involved in IAFP at the national level; most are involved only in their chapter.

Uneven preparation of leadership and annual turnover in chapter leadership leads to lack of continuity and frequent "reinventing of the wheel" syndrome.

A perception exists among members that the election process is not democratic and not open to individual member impact.

IAFP is still perceived by some in the industry to be fighting with other financial planning associations and organizations.

Because of the industry-wide focus, it can be difficult for IAFP to respond appropriately to how various segments are affected by economic and regulatory changes.

Opportunities:

IAFP can help prevent the misuse or inappropriate use of some financial products through education of both consumers and advisers.

IAFP can exert positive, proactive influence on regulatory and legal changes.

IAFP can strengthen our chapters and their ability to serve the education and networking needs of the financial planning community.

IAFP can increase its open forum value through interadvisory council projects of mutual advantage.

IAFP can continue to cooperate with other financial services to help those who are seeking positions in the financial planning industry.

IAFP can develop special interest groups to provide a forum for discussion about the areas of specialization which develop in a maturing industry or profession.

IAFP can develop programs and services which specifically address the needs of beginning, intermediate, and advanced practitioners.

IAFP can develop programs

and services which specifically address the needs of practitioners in solo practice, partnerships, and who work in large organizations.

IAFP can help our members become more successful through training in practice management.

There are 758,500 financial services professionals who are potential members.

The aging population will present increased opportunities for financial advisers.

IAFP can help reduce consumers' confusion about the various designations and qualifications of financial advisers.

IAFP can become a consumer advocate on financial matters.

IAFP can play a major role in educating the public on the value of financial planning.

Threats:

When the financial services industry suffers, those in the industry may be less likely to spend money on Association memberships, products, and services.

Changes in the regulation of financial advisers, tax laws, etc., can discourage financial planners from continuing in the field or make it difficult for them to prosper.

Disreputable/dishonest advisers and product providers associated with financial planning can tarnish the reputation of all.

"Planner bashing" in the media can discourage consumers from seeking professional financial advice.

Misuse or inappropriate use of some financial products can fuel "planner bashing" or lack of public trust in financial planners.

Other associations with clearer identities may attract the primary loyalty of some market segments.

Rising expense may force members to choose between other organizations and IAFP. Changes in tax laws and other rules and regulations can make our products or programs obsolete (audiotapes, for example).

Lack of cooperation with other associations and absence of a "united" professional viewpoint will continue to fuel negative media messages and consumer confusion.

Appendix VI

Goals, Objectives and Strategies

The Academy of General Dentistry (a partial listing)

Goal A: To provide general dentists with the resources and incentives needed to regularly update and expand the dental knowledge and skills they possess.

Objective 1: To implement an in-house audiocassette tape series with a subscription rate of 900 participants by March 31, 1996, and to monitor the retention rate over the next few years.

Strategies:

S1. To actively market the AudioDent series to AGD members with a first brochure mailing by November 30, 1996, and an insert in "Impact" by the Spring of 1996.

S2. To have each member of the DE Council recommend AudioDent topics and moderators annually.

S3. To have an Editorial Board meeting annually to provide input into the educational planning for the AudioDent tapes.

Objective 2: To have 2,500 member subscribers to "Video Journal " by September 1, 1996.

Strategies:

S1. To have an Editorial Board meet at least twice each year to ensure the quality of, and provide the necessary support for, Video Journal

S2. To annually review the Video Journal marketing plans.

Objective 3: To promote the Fellowship award so that the 1996 Fellowship class includes at least 400 Academy members.

Strategies:

S1. To conduct an annual Fellowship orientation seminar during the Academy's annual meeting and at alternative examination sites that would help pre-Fellows understand the FAGD requirements.

S2. To send a series of targeted communications to those pre-Fellows who have completed an advanced educational program or 350 hours of approved continuing dental education by May 1 of each year.

S3. To annually develop printout messages that stimulate member inquiries regarding the FAGD requirements.

S4. To contact rejected Fellowship award applicants to offer help on how to successfully reapply by September 1 of the upcoming year.

S5. To mail a reminder notice on August 1 of each year to all recipients of Fellowship award applications who have not submitted their completed applications to the Chicago office.

Objective 4: To encourage Fellows to pursue the Mastership award so that the 1996 Mastership class includes at least 100 candidates.

Strategies:

S1. To conduct an annual Mastership orientation seminar during the annual meeting to assist Fellows in understanding the Mastership requirements.

S2. To contact rejected Mastership award applicants to offer help on how to successfully reapply by September 1 of the year following rejection.

S3. To mail a reminder notice by August 1 of each year to all recipients of Mastership award applications who have not submitted their completed application to the Chicago office.

S4. To annually develop a printout message that stimulates member inquiries regarding the MAGD requirements.

Objective 5: To help constituents meet the Academy's minimum expectation of offering members access to at least two CE programs in their area or region each year.

Strategies:

S1. To provide a third national video teleconference in 1966.

S2. To market the use of the participation course module with an article in Expectations 2000 in the spring of 1966.

S3. To provide CE planning training at the Biennial Leadership Conference workshop sessions.

S4. To recognize constituents annually who excel in providing exemplary continuing education with CE Awards of Excellence.

Objective 6: To have 90% of the AGD chapters and the intrastate dental ADA components approved by January 1, 1997.

Strategies:

S1. To prepare an article and distribute it annually, to Academy constituent newsletter editors which encourages AGD members to identify their local unapproved components and constituents and assist them to obtain AGD intrastate sponsor approval.

S2. To communicate the need to ensure the approval of intrastate AGD and ADA components to all AGD constituent presidents annually, with copies to the regional directors, CE chairs, and constituent executive secretaries.

Objective 7: To have 90% of the AGD constituent academies approved by the end of each calendar year.

Strategies:

S1. To advise constituent presidents by letter six months prior to their NSAP approval expiration date that they can apply to the Academy's NSAP for renewal.

S2. To assign a member a member of the Committee on National Sponsor Approvals to communicate with the regional director and constituent president of each constituent whose NSAP approval is expiring that the constituent can still utilize the Academy's NSAP program.

Objective 8: To have 95% of the dental schools and ADA constituent societies approved to offer FAGD/MAGD credit at the end of each calendar year.

Strategies:

S1. To encourage the ADA to target the dental schools and ADA constituents whose AGD approval is expiring six months prior to their expiration so that their applications are received prior to the next CERP review.

S2. To assign a member of the Committee on National Sponsor Approvals to each of the dental schools, constituent dental societies, and providers of the major dental meetings whose NASP term is expiring to encourage application to either CERP or the AGD, and thus to ensure continuous FAGD/MAGD credit approval.

S3. To pursue by letter those sponsors who have not applied to either CERP or NASP three months prior to their date of expiration...and encourage that they apply to one of the two approval agencies.

Goal B: To assist general dentists in evaluating dental knowledge and skills.

Objective 1: To have at least 400 AGD members take the Fellowship Examination each year.

Strategies:

S1. To provide press releases concerning the Fellowship Examination to constituent editors and include announcements in the "Uppers & Lowers" newsletter by February 28 of each year.

S2. To market the Examination to pre-Fellows by February 28 of each year in the form of a letter.

S3. To market the exam to all members, including Fellows, as an evaluation tool, by publishing an article in the February issue of "Impact."

S4. To request the editor to include at least three examination announcements/articles highlighting the examination and the reasons for achieving Fellowship in the February, March, and April issues of "Impact."

S5. To provide FAGD examination applicants the option of participating in the "Study-Buddy" plan, by January 1 of each year.

S6. To offer, by March 31 of each year, potential FAGD exam candidates an incentive to take the exam by allowing them to pay half of the annual meeting registration fee.

S7. Beginning with the FAGD Examination of 1992, to incorporate Self-Assessment quiz items into the FAGD Examination.

Objective 2: To sell 600 copies of the FAGD Examination Study Guide in each fiscal year

Strategies:

S1. To include a description of the Study Guide, its purpose, contents, FAGD credits, and price in all articles, announcements and press releases concerning the FAGD Examination by April 30 of each year.

S2. To print a special article highlighting the Study Guide in the February issue of "Impact" each year.

S3. Revise 20% of the Study Guide items by January 1, 1992 and every other year thereafter.

S4. Supply press releases to all dental editors in the Spring about the availability of the Study Guide as a self-instructional tool.

S5. Prepare a case study in the 1996 (4th.) edition of the Study Guide and every other year thereafter.

Goal D: To effectively represent the interests of general dentists in the formulation of public policy.

Objective 1: To ensure that no federal tax legislation that would adversely affect the dental profession is enacted by the Congress prior to the year 2000.

Strategies:

S1. To have the Academy's liaison in Washington, D.C. engage in the following activities on an ongoing basis:

a. Educate Academy members about relevant tax

issues and their implications through articles in various AGD publications within 45 days of their introduction.
b. Develop an action plan within 75 days of the introduction of any relevant tax legislation. Possible activities may include (but not be limited to):

1. Communicating the Academy's position to members of Congress through letters and personal meetings.
2. Participating in those coalitions whose goals regarding specific tax issues parallel those of the Academy.
3. Initiating grass roots campaigns to involve Academy leaders as well as the general membership when appropriate.
4. Monitoring all relevant tax hearings and provide oral or written testimony when appropriate.

Objective 2: To see that the Academy's positions on matters that are the subject of proposed legislation are implemented in every state of the United States within two years of being adopted as Academy policy.

Strategies:
S1. To communicate the Academy's position to Constituent officers within three months following the House of Delegates meeting at which they are adopted.
S2. To have the Academy's positions printed in "Impact" with three months following the House of Delegates meeting each year.
S3. To have the Legislation Council, at its first meeting following any annual meeting, determine in consultation with either the Executive Committee or the Board of Trustees, what, if any, policies should be communicated to constituent academies in the interest of safeguarding the rights of the general dentists concerning issues on which state legislatures may attempt to find solutions.

Objective 3: To have constituent legislative chairpersons appointed in 75% of the constituents, and to have 30% of them conducting measurable legislative activity by September 30, 1996.

Strategies:

S1. To send each new legislative chairperson within two weeks of their appointment a package that outlines his/her duties and available resources.
a. To issue updates to the "Legislative Chairperson's Resource Manual" once each year within 90 days of the Council meeting.

S2. To have a Council member assigned to each new legislative chairperson, and to contact that individual within 30 days of the time the welcome kit is mailed from the Chicago office.

S3. To assign Council members to legislative chairpersons by September 1 annually, and to have them contact each of their chairpersons at least once during the year, by February 28.

S4. To maintain a record of legislative activity for each AGD constituent through a mail/telephone survey to be conducted annually by the AGD staff, with results reported to the Council at its annual spring meeting.

S5. To have Council members contact constituent presidents by April 15 each year when a lack of legislative activity has been identified and when appropriate, to advise the regional director or national trustee of the lack of activity.

S6. To contact legislative chairpersons who attended the legislative breakout session at the Leadership Conference within three weeks of the program in order to offer resources, advice and assistance in planning or implementing legislative activity.

S7. To assist legislative chairpersons in communicating relevant legislative news and in promoting their role as a peer resource to their colleagues through articles in state, constituent, or national AGD publications. At least one communication will be sent to the legislative chairpersons by March 30 each year over the signature of the council chairman.

Objective 4: To have a system of licensure by credentials in place throughout the United States and Canada that will assure freedom of movement for duly licensed dentists in every state and every province by January 1, 2000.

Objective 5: To determine which states and provinces have licensure by credentials as defined by the Academy by using the following activities.

Strategies:

S1. Council members will personally contact their assigned constituents presidents or constituent legislative chairs by April 15, 1995, to notify them that the Chicago staff will be mailing a survey ...

S2. That survey, that will be mailed by May 15, 1995, will include, as a background statement, the Academy's current definition of licensure by credentials, as well as the House resolution prompting the inquiry.

S3. After 30 days, Council members will contact those AGD constituents who have not responded to the survey.

S4. That survey will be used by the Council at its meetings in Fall 1995 and Spring 1996 to determine which constituents want support from the Academy and in what form.

S5. To offer those constituents by December 31, 1996, requesting assistance, help in promoting licensure by credentials information that will fulfill their request and help them convince their state or provincial dental association and state or provincial boards of dental examiners to pursue licensure by credentials.

Appendix VII

Goals, Objectives and Strategies

Door and Hardware Institute (a partial listing)

Goal 1: Develop and maintain a widely accepted credentialing system based on competence, and encourage ethical compliance.

Objective 1A: Evaluate the DHI certification program against future member skill needs. Completion date, 7-1-95.
Strategy 1A-1: Survey consultant and apprentice members by 7-1-95 to determine their future skills needs as well as their opinion of the credibility of the current program.
Tactic 1A-1a: Draft a questionnaire with assistance of the Board of Certification...by 4-1-95.
Tactic 1A-1b: Identify and secure approval of funding by 4-7-95.
Tactic 1A-1c: Mail survey on 4-15-95 with return deadline date of 5-15-95.
Tactic 1A-1d: Complete survey results by 7-1-95.

Objective 1B: Adjust the DHI certification program to fit emerging needs. Completion date, 7-1-95.
Strategy 1B-1: Develop a white paper on the re-

commended adjustments to the DHI certification program to be presented for approval to the Board of Directors at their 5/96 meeting. The paper will contain the suggested dates for the adjustment to the program.

Tactic 1B-1a: Analyze research data and prepare recommendations for adjustments to the program by 10-1-95.

Tactic 1B-1b: Present recommended adjustments to other stakeholders (architects, spec writers, code officials, fire marshals, DHI council chairs) for validation/input by 2-1-96.

Tactic 1B-1c: Present final adjustments for approval to BOC at 2/96 meeting. Appoint Task Force for 1B-1D.

Tactic 1B-1d: Review the process for testing the competency of certification applicants by 3-1-96.

Tactic 1B-1e: Produce final white paper addressing competency, program adjustments and completion dates by 4-1-96.

Tactic 1B-1f: Present white paper at 5-96 board meeting and secure approval of adjustments and implementation deadline dates.

Tactic 1B-1g: Prepare budget by 8-1-96.

Tactic 1B-1h: BOC reviews guidelines for ethical compliance at its 8/96 meeting and makes recommendations to Board of Directors for their fall meeting.

Tactic 1B-1i: Board of Directors to approve adjustments at 10-96 meeting.

Tactic 1B-1j: All adjustments implemented by 5-1-97.

Objective 1C: Develop a process to encourage compliance with DHI credentialing standards. Completion date, 5-1-97.

Strategy 1C-1: Develop a communication vehicle to encourage participation in and compliance with the new DHI credentialing standards by 5-1-97.

Tactic 1C-1a: Determine the appropriate vehicles and develop budgets for encouraging compliance with credentialing standards by 1-1-97.

Tactic 1C-1b: Implement the credentialing communication and marketing process by 5-1-97.

Objective 1D: Develop a public information/ promotion program to increase the perceived value of the DHI credentialing program. Completion date, 1-1-96.

Strategy 1D-1: Utilize the marketing plan developed under Goal 2 and the two-way communication process under the Cultural Goal to promote the value of the DHI credentialing program.

Goal 2: Serve as an effective voice in advocating the industry's interests with important stakeholders (individuals, manufacturers, sales agencies, distributors, government, architects, customers, etc.)

Objective 2A: Identify and evaluate stakeholders who are important to DHI and its members. Completion date, 8-1-95.

Strategy 2A-1: Conduct a staff review to identify and prioritize stakeholders of importance to our industry by 4-1-95.

Tactic 2A-1a: Review the 1993 Membership Critical Issues Study to identify and prioritize stakeholders. Validate with DHI volunteers and produce a prioritized list of stakeholders by 4-1-95.

Strategy 2A-2: Review current relationships with important stakeholders and their associations through staff and leadership interviews and surveys by 6-1-95.

Tactic 2A-2a: Complete staff interviews evaluating DHI's relationship with important stakeholders by 4-1-95.

Tactic 2A-2b: Survey DHI's leadership (Board of Directors and Councils) to identify and evaluate ongoing liaisons with stakeholders by 5-1-95.

Tactic 2A-2c: Produce a report summarizing DHI's relationships with important stakeholders by 6-1-95.

Strategy 2A-3: Identify areas of mutual interest with each stakeholder by 8-1-95.

Tactic 2A-3a: Complete interviews of staff to determine areas of mutual interest by 4-1-95.

Tactic 2A-3b: Complete interviews with DHI leadership to determine areas of mutual interest by 6-1-95.

Tactic 2A-3c: Complete interviews with stakeholder associations' staff to determine areas of mutual interest by 8-1-95.

Objective 2B: Establish optimal relationships with each important stakeholder. Identify vehicles for advocacy with each stakeholder. Completion date, 1-1-96.
Strategy 2B-1: Identify appropriate vehicle for communicating with each important stakeholder by 8-1-95.
Tactic 2B-1a: Conduct interviews with stakeholders/associations to identify vehicles by 8-1-95.
Strategy 2B-2: Utilize identified vehicles for advocacy starting on 1-1-96.
Tactic 2B-2a: Develop an advocacy marketing plan and budget for 1996 fiscal year by 8-1-95.
Tactic 2B-2b: Receive approval for advocacy budget by 11-1-95.
Tactic 2B-2c: Develop advocacy material and implement marketing plan by 1-1-96.

Objective 2C: Maintain ongoing two-way communications with all stakeholders starting on 9-1-95.

Strategy 2C-1: Staff will maintain ongoing two-way communications with stakeholders utilizing volunteer leadership as appropriate by 9-1-95.
Tactic 2C-1a: Assign responsibilities for staff liaison or volunteer liaison with stakeholders by 6-1-95.
Tactic 2C-1b: Evaluate and update EVP quarterly on communication with stakeholders.

Goal 3: Serve as the principle resource for professional development in the door, hardware, specialty, and security products industry.

Objective 3A: Conduct ongoing assessment of member professional development needs in management, sales, marketing, technical, and leadership training. Completion date, 6-1-96.
Strategy 3A-1: Establish volunteer/staff teams to oversee development and implementation of professional development objectives by 6-1-95.
Tactic 3A-1a: Technical Education: establish a

new technical education task force of AHI instructors, council members, and BOC members by 6-1-95.
Tactic 3A-1b: Management Education: assemble a new management education task force of council members and AHI instructors by 6-1-95.
Tactic 3A-1c: Leadership Training: assemble a new leadership training task force of select manufacturer personnel, chapter presidents and board members by 6-1-95.
Strategy 3A-2: Through surveys and focus groups assess members' professional development needs by 6-1-96.
Tactic 3A-2a: Review results of the convention distributor education survey by 6-1-95.
Tactic 3A-2b: Review and analyze the consultant survey produced under program goal 1, objective 1A and decide on the steps to be taken based on results by 6-1-95.
Tactic 3A-2c: Work with Task Forces to develop educational survey topics by 2-1-96.
Tactic 3A-2d: Develop budget for 1996 industry education survey by 8-1-95.
Tactic 3A-2e: Finalize survey at councils convention meeting, 1-1-96.
Tactic 3A-2f: Mail the survey to targeted audiences by 2-1-96 with a response deadline of 2-28-96.
Tactic 3A-2g: Compile results of survey by 4-15-96.
Tactic 3A-2h: produce analysis of results by 6-1-96.

Objective 3B: Identify and develop programs that address member professional development needs in management, sales, marketing, technical, and leadership training. Completion date, 9-1-96.
Strategy 3B-1: Identify and review current educational programs, and compare to the results of above survey by 8-1-96.
Tactic 3B-1a: In current marketing materials for educational programs, include notice that these programs have been requested by members.
Strategy 3B-2: Based on the program review, develop a preliminary budget by 8-1-96 and complete preliminary development of new programs based on member needs by 9-1-96.

Objective 3C: Develop cost-effective delivery mechanisms for professional development programs in management, sales, marketing, technical, and leadership training. Completion date, 6-1-97.

Strategy 3C-1: Identify potential delivery mechanisms by 12-1-96.

Strategy 3C-2: Determine the most cost-effective delivery mechanisms by 5-1-97.

Tactic 3C-2a: Analyze costs of potential delivery mechanisms by 3-1-97, including partnerships with outside skills training sources.

Tactic 3C-2b: Secure validation of a sample group of potential programs through focus groups by 4-1-97.

Objective 3D: Implement new professional development programs in management, sales, marketing, technical, and leadership training. Completion date, 6-1-98.

Strategy 3D-1: Develop a schedule, budget and work plan for implementing the new professional development programs by 12-1-97.

Strategy 3D-2: Complete the development of new professional development programs in each field by 6-1-98.

Appendix VIII

Goals, Objectives and Strategies

National Center for Missing and Exploited Children (a partial listing)

Goal 1: Find missing children.

Objective 1: Find out more about non-family abduction (NFA), family abduction (FA), and lost, injured, and other missing (LIM) cases. Increase the number of NFA, FA, and LIM case intakes by 100% by 1-1-98.

Objective 2: Find out more about NFA, FA, and LIM cases quicker. Reduce notification time by 50% by 1-1-98.

Strategies for Objectives 1 and 2:

1. In partnership with the FBI, advocate an amendment to the National Child Search Assistance Act of 1990 to mandate an NCIC check off identifying "endangered juvenile" cases, providing rapid notification to the FBI and NCMEC.
2. Complete NCMEC's national missing children's network. Create clearinghouses in three

remaining states.
3. Increase awareness of NCMEC through articles in major police publications, roll call training videos, and newsletters.
4. Promote and create universal awareness of NCMEC's hotline, 1-800-THE-LOST to law enforcement, media, and the general public.
5. Promote NCMEC for case reports and leads through the online services and the Internet.
6. Increase the number of local police agencies on the NCMEC computer network.
7. Maximize networking between the NCMEC branches and law enforcement agencies in their regions to encourage prompt case notification.

Objective 3: Improve the recovery rate in NFA, FA, and LIM cases to 90% of cases in intake by 1-1-99.

Strategies for Objective 3:
Expand Project ALERT.
2. Enhance NCMEC's case analysis function to provide more in-depth assistance in more cases.
3. Enhance NCMEC technology tools, including the implementation of expert systems, artificial intelligence, and facial matching.
4. Develop expanded dissemination of images and information via television.
5. Increase the number of national photo partners.
6. Enhance NCMEC legal technical assistance available to parents, law enforcement, attorneys, and prosecutors.
7. Provide training and updated resources to branches to enhance their effectiveness in supporting NCMEC and law enforcement.

Objective 4: Increase the rate of location of children in cases of international child abduction to 75% of cases by 1-1-98.

Strategies for Objective 4:
1. Establish an Inter-national Division.
2. Create a "Children's INTERPOL," linking NCMEC with law enforcement and child advocacy organizations worldwide.

Objective 5: Prepare 10 million American families to respond effectively in the event that their child ever becomes missing by providing free tools and information by 1-1-97.

Strategies for Objective 5:

1. Aggressively promote NCMEC's free materials and brochures for families, including "Just in Case...Parental guidelines in case your child might someday be missing," through family-oriented media.
2. Aggressively promote NCMEC's child identification programs including KidCare and Kidprint, to children and families through encouraging stories and feature articles in family-oriented media.
3. Support branch initiatives for outreach and participation in child safety programs in their regions.

Objective 6: Provide free KidCare ID's to ten million children by 1-1-97.

Strategies for Objective 6:

1. Aggressively market and promote KidCare to prospective private and public sector sponsors on a local and national basis.
2. Encourage law enforcement agencies to incorporate KidCare into existing child safety and crime prevention programs.
3. Promote linkages, tie-ins and cross-promotions with the organization's other projects and activities.
4. Recognize, support, and seek to maintain the involvement of existing sponsors.
5. Increase the number of endorsements, including law enforcement and educational organizations, unions, and civic groups.
6. Explore database development from voluntary capture of names and addresses of KidCare participants.

Objective 7: Implement a national electronic, "Have You Seen Me?" network by 7-1-98.

Strategies for Objective 7:

1. Place multimedia kiosks for the transmission of images and information in high traffic locations — i.e., airports and malls.
2 Promote kiosk sponsorships as advertising, offering sponsors visibility in high traffic locations linked to a compelling cause for a competitive cost.

3. Create a national television capability to quickly transmit images and information in breaking cases via satellite.

Objective 8: Increase professional awareness. Conduct targeted training for law enforcement and other professionals in 12 states by 1-1-97.

Strategies for Objective 8:
1. Provide support to the Fox Valley/Basic Investigator's Course (BITMAC).
2. Conduct NCMEC's Infant Abduction Prevention Training for hospitals in targeted states.

Objective 9: Establish a stronger relationship with credible non-profit service providers currently meeting OJJDP/NCMEC criteria by offering direct support to victims and their families.

Strategies for Objective 9:
1. Survey and assess, on an ongoing basis, services currently offered by the 39 credible service providers in the United States, Canada, and Europe currently meeting OJJDP/NCMEC criteria in order to build a resource and referral network for victims and families.
2. Continue to provide training and technical assistance to all NPOs located throughout the country to better ensure the appropriate handling of missing child cases.

Objective 10: Maintain and expand a case management program to target cases more than two years old, utilizing imaging to generate new leads and keep cases alive.

Strategies for Objective 10:
1. Increase technology support to NCMECs age progression laboratory.
2. Maintain and expand a computer network linking NCMEC imaging personnel and technology with forensic artists in key geographic regions and to provide training for these artists in the use of the system to enable more cases to be addressed and greater technology application.
3. Aggressively promote long-term cases in order to increase media exposure.

Goal 2: Prevent child victimization and exploitation

Objective 1: Change the behavior of children and parents through education. Persuade the other 35 states to mandate by law the implementation of child protection curricula meeting NCMEC-recommended standards in every elementary school in the state.

Objective 2: Offer "Kids & Company: Together for Safety" as a model curriculum for potential selection and use by states.

Strategies for Objectives 1 and 2:

1. Develop and promote model child protection curriculum mandate legislation for states.
2. For those state expressing interest in "Kids & Company," develop and present a model based upon the experience of the Commonwealth of Massachusetts and the State of New York.
3. Conduct fund-raising through foundations, corporations and local events to raise funds to place "Kids & Company" in schools in states and communities where there is a demonstrated interest.

Objective 3: Reach targeted audiences with the most effective, usable child protection materials possible.

1. Write and publish a comprehensive child protection guide for families, a readable, usable, "Dr. Spock-type" reference book.
2. Produce and distribute a crisp, effective child protection video for in-home use.
3. Develop targeted, effective materials for teenagers, the single most victimized segment of the U.S. population.

Objective 4: Establish an Exploited Child Unit to provide state and local law enforcement with technical, technological, and professional support in the areas of child molestation, child pornography and child prostitution by 1-1-97.

Strategies for Objective 4:

1. Expand NCMEC's Advocacy Division to

work more aggressively on legislative changes.

2. Identify and acquire applied technology tools, including automatic facial matching to assist state and local law enforcement in the identification of facial images from confiscated child pornography.

Objective 5:
(1) Promote the use of NCMEC's National Child Pornography Tipline.
(2) Launch an awareness campaign regarding NCMEC's National Child Pornography Tipline for users of computer online services and the Internet.

Objective 6: Create a climate to identify and isolate offenders. Achieve the adoption of NCMEC's state sex offender strategy in ten states by 1-1-97.

Objective 7: Deter offenders and prospective offenders. Achieve the enactment of sex offender registration laws in the remaining four states by 1-1-97.

Objective 8: Establish a system allowing community notification regarding the release of dangerous offenders. Achieve the enactment of community notification laws in the remaining 21 states by 1-1-97.

Strategies for Objectives 4, 5, and 6:

1. Promote NCMEC's "Report Card to the Nation," legislative support role, model legislation, publications, and technical assistance to elected officials in key states.
2. Issue and annual "Report Card to the Nation," upgrading progress in child protection law and policy nationally and state-by-state.
3. Promote NCMEC as an expert resource to testify or appear with governors or attorney generals to announce or support legislation.
4. Create and disseminate a Community Notification guide for state and communities to help them implement community notification programs in a positive, reasonable, effective manner.

Goal 4: Create organizational awareness.

Objective 1: Improve public recognition and awareness of the organization. Increase name, logo, and organizational awareness by 20% over the level measured...in 1995, by 7-1-97.

Strategies for Objective 1:

1. Identify a credible market or survey research organization which will include a question(s) on a survey instrument measuring name and log recognition at a no-cost or low-cost basis.
2. Develop major media opportunities for exposure of the organization as an "expert" resource regarding missing and exploited children.
3. Develop targeted media opportunities in family-oriented publications and programs, focusing upon Goal 3, Prevention of Child Victimization.
4. Develop grassroots media opportunities for exposure of the organization on actual cases and on prevention messages.
5. Develop media opportunities for exposure of the organization in education and law enforcement-related trade and association publications.

Objective 2: Create greater national awareness of the nature, seriousness, and extent of the problem of family abduction.

Strategy for Objective 2:

1. Launch public education and awareness campaign in partnership with the U.S. Department of Justice and leading organizations, including the American Bar Association, the National District Attorneys Association, the National Association of Attorneys General, etc., with a prominent, visible spokesperson.

Appendix IX

Goals, Objectives and Strategies

National Head Start Association

Goal 1: To provide a unified national voice for the membership of NHSA and the Head Start community.

Objectives:

1.1. By 9-30-96, NHSA will develop a process for establishing affiliations between itself and each state and regional Head Start association.

1.2. By 9-30-97, 75% of all state and regional Head Start associations will become affiliate associations of NHSA.

1.3. By 9-30-2000, 100% of all state and regional Head Start associations will become affiliate associations of NHSA.

1.4. By 9-30-96, NHSA will have established all policies necessary to enable it to provide a unified national voice for its membership and will have devised a plan for evaluating the implementation and execution of these policies.

1.5. By 9-30-96, NHSA will have developed a comprehensive public relations program that will ensure uniformity in informing the general public about Head Start issues.

1.6. By 9-30-2000, NHSA will have provided all members of its board of directors and presidents of affiliated regional and state associations with ongoing training about their roles and responsibilities to ensure the provision of a unified national voice for NHSA membership and the Head Start community.

1.7. By 3-1-96, and each year thereafter through 3-1-2000, NHSA will determine its goals for impacting on the Head Start program and will disseminate them to all members and to all state and regional associations.

Goal 2: To attain a membership base which is large and diverse enough to support the mission of NHSA.

Objectives:

2.1. By 9-30-96, NHSA will develop a comprehensive membership services plan based on an empirical assessment of the needs and wants of its membership which will govern the provision of services designed to meet the most important of these needs and wants.

2.2. In the period extending from 10-1-96 through 9-30-2000, NHSA will annually retain 90% of the preceding year's membership.

2.3. By 8-30-96, NHSA will develop a comprehensive membership marketing plan designed to produce a 15% increase in each category of membership during each year in the period extending from 10-1-96 through 9-30-2000.

2.4. To address ways to better meet NHSA's current publication demands.

Goal 3: To act as a catalyst to influence federal legislation and policies that positively impact the Head Start Program and poor children and families.

Objectives:

3.1. By 11-1-95, NHSA will develop a written plan to maximize the coordination of internal association resources toward the achievement of legislative goals which will serve the needs of its members.

3.2. By 12-1-95, and each year thereafter through 12-1-2000, NHSA will develop a written legislative work plan that will guide its legislative activities for the next calendar year.

3.3. By 12-30-96, NHSA will develop a plan for enhancing its capacity to conduct field activities designed to educate and involve its membership and the Head Start community in the federal leg-

islative process. Minimally, the plan will address the following issues:
- the organization of the Government Affairs Division required to enhance capacity in this area
- position descriptions of the staff members charged with enhancing this capacity
- staffing levels required to enhance this capacity

3.4. By 1-30-96, NHSA will hire at least one additional staff member in the area of government affairs in order to enhance its capacity to conduct field activities as outlined in the plan referenced above.
3.5. By 1-30-96, NHSA will develop and disseminate an information packet which will inform congressional staff persons about the services, resources, and support NHSA can provide to them.
3.6. Between 6-30-96 and 6-30-2000, NHSA will annually offer training and technical assistance on legislative processes and voter registration to at least ten state and regional Head Start associations.

Goal 4: To develop the capacity of NHSA to impact on legislation beneficial to its members at the state level.

Objectives:
4.1. By 1-96, each state Head Start association will designate a "point person" who will collaborate with NHSA to develop this capacity.
4.2. By 7-96, NHSA will have identified the appropriate training topics for assisting state associations to develop this capacity.
4.3. Between 10-1-96 and 9-30-98, NHSA will offer training and outreach services designed to develop this capacity to all "point persons" designated by state Head Start associations and to other members of these associations who desire and can access this training.
4.4. By 7-96, NHSA will complete a study of the feasibility of establishing regional offices which will assist regional and state associations to develop this capacity.

Goal 5: To establish national and state organizational partnerships which will benefit poor children and families and are consistent with the mission of NHSA.

Objectives:
5.1: By 10-1-98, NHSA will enhance its ability to

impact on partnership activities on the national level which benefit its members. This strategy will include:
- development of a template to analyze existing partnerships
- development and nurturing of appropriate relationships with similar national organizations,...and dissemination to all classes of membership
- tactics for increasing the influence of NHSA on collaborative and transition projects
- a plan for annual year-end evaluations of existing partnerships
- by 6-1-97, NHSA will establish an internally-funded partnership office which has the capacity to address these critical needs
- by 10-1-97, NHSA will have developed the capacity to assist regional and state associations in fostering partnerships
- the designation of "point persons" by state and regional associations who will collaborate with NHSA to develop this capacity
- by 10-1-97, NHSA will have established a technical assistance program which will enable regional and state associations to develop effective partnerships.

5.2. By 6-1-97, NHSA will establish an internally-funded partnership office which has the capacity to address these critical needs.

5.3. By 10-1-97, NHSA will have developed the capacity to assist regional and state associations in fostering partnerships. This capacity will include:
- The designation of "point persons" by state and regional associations who will collaborate with NHSA to develop this capacity.
- By 10-1-97, NHSA will have established a technical assistance program which will enable regional and state associations to develop effective partnerships.

5.4. By 10-1-98, NHSA will have made at least two other special efforts designed to further advance its role as a shaper of the national agenda for poor children and families while partnering with other key national players.

5.5. By 7-96, NHSA will have completed a feasibility study about the establishment of a Head Start children's foundation.

Goal 6: To provide high quality training for Head Start staff and parents which will enable them to develop professionally and personally.

Objectives:

6.1. Starting in 12-95, NHSA will biannually sponsor focus groups at all its conferences and assess the future training needs of staff and parents.
6.2. By 3-96, NHSA will make available to parents and staff written, up-to-date factual materials that will enable them to serve as effective and consistent advocates for the Head Start Program.
6.3. By 5-96, NHSA will have explored the feasibility of providing parent members of the association with a periodical that supports their role as the primary educators of their children beyond Head Start and into their children's primary grade years. If the project is deemed feasible, the first issue will be published by 12-96.
6.4. By 10-1-96, NHSA and ACYF will formulate a collaborative agreement outlining their respective responsibilities in the areas of leadership and component training for Head Start parents and staff which will be effective for the period extending from 10-96 to 9-2000.
6.5. Starting in 12-96, NHSA will use information derived from the biannual conference-based focus groups to formulate the content of future conferences sponsored by the association.
6.6. By 10-1-97, NHSA will have identified major wellness issues of concern to its members, such as stress management, and will have formulated a mode Employee Assistance Program responsive to these concerns, which can be implemented through the staff development process.
6.7. By 10-1-2000, at least 33% of all member agencies will be offering the model Employee Assistance Program devised by the association.

Goal 7: To assure that all Head Start programs receive the technical assistance and support they require to deliver high quality services.

Objectives:

7.1. By 1-30-96, and each 1-30 thereafter until the year 2000, NHSA will gather information from its membership and other sources regarding the members' needs for technical assistance.
7.2. By 3-31-96 and each 3-31 thereafter until the year

2000, NHSA will prioritize these needs for technical assistance, formulate a plan, and allocate resources for meeting these prioritized needs during the next 12-month period.

7.3. Between 3-31-96 and 3-31-2000, the period in which assistance plans will be implemented, ongoing consideration should be given to the development of distance learning capabilities which will support the association's efforts to offer technical assistance to its members.

7.4. During each year in the period extending from 3-31-96 through 3-31-2000, NHSA will evaluate the content of its technical assistance and support systems and the processes of delivering these services at least once every quarter.

7.5. Once each year in the period extending from 10-1-96 through 9-30-2000, NHSA will request assistance from private industry to evaluate its use of technology and provide expertise on maximizing this use.

Goal 8: To provide leadership and advocacy for the development of applied research that will provide accurate information about the Head Start Program and support the delivery of high quality services to the Head Start community.

Objectives:

8.1. By 12-30-96, NHSA will secure linkages with five additional organizations and institutions in the research community and, as a result, increase its influence in the area of applied research.

8.2. By 12-30-97, NHSA will complete an assessment of the research environment which will enable it to determine the applied research needs of its members and the Head Start community.

8.3. By 3-30-98, NHSA will develop an agenda for applied research beneficial to its members and the Head Start community and disseminate it to organizations interested in and capable of this type of research.

8.4. Beginning in 3-2000, NHSA will foster implementation of priorities found beneficial by research that will result in improved services to Head Start children and families.

Appendix X

Implementation Plan

National Head Start Association (Goal 1 Only)

Goal 1:
Objective 1.1: By 9-30-96, NHSA will develop a process for establishing affiliations between itself and each State and Regional Head Start Association.

Milestones	Tactics	Date	Staff/ Resources
1.1.1 Gather baseline information about other organizations to describe what a model affiliation process looks like.	- identify three national organizations that have affiliate structures - identify information needed regarding affiliation process - obtain information from the three about affiliation process - review and determine if more information is needed - analyze and create profile affiliation process	11-10- 95	PP
1.1.2: Develop baseline information regarding structure, membership, and operations of each state and regional association	- determine what information is already available about each state and regional association	11-10-95	R&E

	- determine information needed	11-30- 95	Mgmt. R&E
	- develop interview format	1-22-96	R&E
	- interview state/regional presidents	1-30-96	R&E GAP PP
	- prepare profiles of each state and regional association	4-30- 96	R&E
1.1.3: Prepare written process for state and regional affiliation for board approval	- from 1.1.2 information, outline content of affiliation process	6-28- 96	Dep. PP
	- design NHSA affiliation model	8-16- 96	Mgmt.
	- submit to board for approval	9-1-96	

Objective 1.2. By 9-30-97, 75% of all state and regional Head Start associations will become affiliate associations of NHSA.

1.2.1: 25% affiliated	- presentation to state and regional presidents	1-31- 97	CEO PM
	- develop affiliate membership package		PM
	- disseminate materials		PM GAD CEO
	- monitor and T/TA - status reports		
1.2.2: 50 % affiliated	- monitor and T/TA - status reports	5-30- 97	GAD CEO
1.2.3: 75% affiliated	- monitor and T/TA - status report	9-30- 97	GAD CEO

Objective 1.3: By 9-30-2000, 100% of state and regional associations will be NHSA affiliates.

1.3.1: 100% state affiliation-	- same as 1.2.	9-30- 00	see 1.2
1.3.2: 100% regional affiliation-	- same as 1.2	9-30- 00	see 1.2

Objective 1.4: By 9-30-96, NHSA will have established all policies necessary to enable it to provide a unified national voice for its membership and will have devised a plan for evaluating the implementation and execution of these policies.

1.4.1: Determine what policies are necessary	- poll membership for recommendations on providing unified voice	1-30- 96	Dep. PP
	- poll other advocacy organizations for what policies they use to create a unified voice	1-30- 96	GAD

	- compile information and prepare policy index	2-28-96	R&E
	- recommend policies	3-15-96	Mgmt.
1.4.2: Prepare written policies for board	- draft policies	4-20-96	PM
	- determine design and format for each policy	4-30-96	PM
	- obtain feedback from selected Head Start community	6-15-96	GAD PP
	- to board for approval	9-30-96	CEO
1.4.3: Implement and evaluate policies	- staff orientation.	10-30-96	CEO
	develop packages of policies and samples	1-10-97	PP
	- board and presidents orientation	1-25-97	CEO GAD R&E
	- prepare evaluation	2-30-97	

Objective 1.5: By 9-30-96, NHSA will have developed a comprehensive public relations program that will ensure uniformity in informing the general public about Head Start issues.

1.5.1 Poll members	- poll members to determine general feelings regarding past PR efforts	1-30-96	DD
1.5.2 Assess PR firms and other sources	- determine PR firms and other avenues to be used to inform public of Head Start issues	4-30-96	DD
1.5.3 Contract with PR firm	- contract with PR firm	10-1-95	DD
1.5.4 PR firm will provide input	- PR firm will provide services in writing, issues papers, discussion with media, provide training to local programs and state associations	7-30-96	DD
1.5.5 Assess compliance with goal	- review PR efforts and through use of newspaper and other media services	9-30-96	DD

Objective 1.6: By 9-30-2000, NHSA will provide all members of its Board of Directors and presidents of its affiliated state and regional associations with the ongoing training about their roles and responsibilities to ensure the provision of a unified national voice for NHSA membership and the Head Start community.

1.6.1 Ongoing training at state and regional president's meeting and as needed by field representatives.	- work with CEO and president to develop training materials in the areas of grassroots organizing, legislation, partnership, and advocacy	ongoing	R&E PP GAD DD

Objective 1.7: By 3-1-96, and each year thereafter through 3-1-2000, NHSA will determine its goals for impacting on the Head Start program and will disseminate them to all members and to all state and regional associations.

1.7.1 To address and identify issues both legislative and otherwise	- monitor Congressional activities - inform NHSA board, state and regional presidents and membership through updates, mailings, and electronic devices	ongoing	PR GAD

LEGEND:

R&E = Research and Evaluation
PP = Partnership Project
GAD = Government Affairs Division
DD = Deputy Director
CEO = Chief Executive Officer
PM = Publishing and Marketing
Tech = Technology Department
Firm = Consulting Firm
Mgmt. = Management Team: all of the above

Appendix XI

Strategic Planning Schedule

The American Pharmaceutical Association

January 1996

At its planning retreat, the APhA Board of Trustees will:

- approve 1996 planning schedule
- validate and/or revise the "APhA 2000" vision statement
- briefly review accomplishments in achieving 1995 goals and objectives (via CEO's final report to the CEO Evaluation Committee)
- receive and act upon the 1996 CEO objectives as recommended by the CEO Evaluation Committee
- review changes in the internal and external environments that have occurred in the past year and which are predicted for the future
- in preparation for the development of additional 1997 preliminary Association objectives, discuss, revise, supplement, categorize, and prioritize the list of possible 1996 strategies, tactics, programs, and new business opportunities developed in the course of the 1996 strategic planning process

April, 1996

- during APhA academies' Leadership Weekend, academy leaders discuss and recommend actions and/or revisions to the prioritized list of suggested 1997 strategies, tactics, programs, and new business opportunities developed by the Board of Trustees at its January retreat

May, 1996

- Ad Hoc Planning Group meets to develop a draft of 1997 Association goals and objectives based on the categorization and prioritization of the above by Board of Trustees and Academy leaders
- Board of Trustees approves draft of 1997 Association goals and 1996 preliminary Association objectives for use in initial work by staff in developing 1996 work plans and budget
- Board of Trustees reviews mid-year progress on accomplishment of 1996 Association goals and objectives

September, 1996

- Ad Hoc Planning Group meets to develop recommendations to the Board of Trustees on: 1) a final draft of 1997 Association goals; 2) a final draft of 1997 Association objectives with recommendation for prioritization; and, 3) possible 1998 Association strategies, tactics, programs, and new business opportunities to be used for the development of 1998 Association preliminary objectives
- Board of Trustees approves final draft of 1997 Association goals
- Board of Trustees approves final draft and prioritizes 1997 Association objectives
- Board of Trustees holds preliminary discussion of 1998 Association strategies, tactics, programs, and new business opportunities that will serve as the basis for the drafting of the 1998 Association preliminary objectives
- focus groups of state executives held during the APhA Affiliated State Pharmacy Association Executives meeting provide input on 1997 Association goals and objectives

September-October, 1996

- staff develops final draft of 1997 CEO objectives and develops staff work plans to achieve 1997 Association and CEO objectives

November, 1996

- Board of Trustees reviews draft 1997 CEO objectives and provides input to CEO Evaluation Committee
- Board of Trustees approves 1997 staff work plans through approval of the 1997 Association budget
- Board of Trustees continues its preliminary discussion of possible 1998 Association strategies, tactics, programs, and new business opportunities which will serve as the basis for the development of 1998 Association preliminary objectives

Bibliography

Bettinger, Cass. "Use Corporate Culture to Trigger High Performance." *Journal of Business Strategy*, 10, no.2 (March/April, 1989): 38-42.

Bryson, John M. Strategic Planning for Public and Non-Profit Organizations. San Francisco: Jossey-Bass, 1990.

Carlzon, Jan. Moments of Truth. New York: Ballinger Publishing Company, 1987.

Dalziel, M. and Schoonover, S. Changing Ways: A Practical Tool for Implementing Change Within Organizations. New York: American Management Association, 1988.

Drucker, Peter F. Management: Tasks, Responsibilities, Practices. New York: Harper and Row Publishers, 1973.

Eadie, Douglas C. "Strategic Issues Management: Building an Organization's Strategic Capability." *Economic Development Commentary*, 11, no. 3 (Fall 1987): 18-21. (Washington, D.C.: Council for Urban Economic Development.)

Eadie, Douglas C. and Steinbacher, R. "Strategic Agenda Management: A Marriage of Organizational Development and Strategic Planning." *Public Administration Review* 45 (1985): 424-30.

Espy, Siri N. Handbook of Strategic Planning for Non-Profits. New York: Praeger, 1986.

Farnham, A., "State Your Values. Hold The Hot Air," *Fortune*, vol. 127 (April 19, 1993): 117-118.

Freeman, R.E. Strategic Management: A Stakeholder's Approach. Boston: Pitman, 1984.

Hambrick, D.C. "Environmental Scanning and Organizational Strategy." *Strategic Management Journal* 3, no. 2 (1982): 159-74.

Hamel, G. and Prahalad, C.K. *Harvard Business Review*, vol. 71 (March 14, 1993): 75-84.

Hutchings, Vicki and Lewis, John. "Battle for Planning Power Heats Up." *New Statesman and Society*, vol 1, no. 28 (December 16, 1988): 24-25.

Jarratt, J., Coates, J., Mahaffie, J., and Hines, A. Managing Your Future as an Association: Thinking About Trends and Working With Their Consequences, 1994-2020. Washington, D.C.: The American Society of Association Executives Foundation, 1994.

Kakis, Frederick J. "Applying Strategic Planning." *Business Insurance*, July 6, 1990, 20.

Lab, R. Competitive Strategic Management. Englewood Cliffs, New Jersey: Prentice-Hall, 1984.

Manzini, Andrew O. and Gridley, John D. Integrating Human Resources and Strategic Business Planning. New York: AMACOM, 1986.

Mason, R. and Mitroff, I. Challenging Strategic Planning Assumptions. New York: Wiley, 1982.

Mintzberg, H., "The Fall and Rise of Strategic Planning." *Harvard Business Review*, vol. 72 (January/February, 1994): 110-114.

Nutt, P.C. and Backoff, R.W. "A Strategic Management Process for Public and Third-Sector Organizations." *Journal of the American Planning Association* 53 (1987): 53, 44-57.

Oster, Sharon. Strategic Management for Non-Profit Organizations: Theory and Cases. New York: Oxford University Press, 1995.

Pennings, J., ed. Strategic Decision Making in Complex Organizations. San Francisco: Jossey-Bass, 1985.

Peters, Thomas J. and Waterman, R.H. In Search of Excellence: Lessons from America's Best Run Companies. New York: Harper and Row, 1982.

Plaum, A. and Delmont, T. "External Scanning: A Tool for Planners." *Journal of the American Planning Association* 53, no. 1 (1987): 56-67.

Quigley, Joseph V. Vision: How Leaders Can Develop It, Share It, Sustain *It*. New York: McGraw-Hill, 1993.

Ring, P.S. and Perry, J.L. "Strategic Management in Public and Private Organizations." *Academy of Management Review* 10 (1985): 276-86.

Rowe, Alan J., et al. Strategic Management: A Methodological Approach. Reading, Mass.: Addison-Wesley, 1989.

Rue, L.W. and Holland, P.G. Strategic Management: Concepts and Experiences. New York: McGraw-Hill, 1986.

Sandy, William. "Avoid the Breakdowns Between Planning and Implementation." *Journal of Business Strategy*, September/October, 1991, 30-33.

Shaw, John C. The Service Focus: Developing Winning Game Plans for Service Companies. Homewood, Illinois: Dow-Jones-Irwin, 1990.

Taylor, B. "Strategic Planning: Which Style Do You Need?" *Long-Range Planning* 17 (1984): 51-62.

Tregoe, Benjamin, B. and Tobia, Peter M. "An Action-Oriented Approach to Strategy." *Journal of Business Strategy* 11, no. 1 (January/February 1990): 16.

Yanes, W.B. "What in the World is Likely to Affect Your Market?: Environmental Scanning Keeps Companies Abreast of Sociological Changes That Could Influence Their Business." *Investor's Daily*, September 14, 1990, 8.

ADDITIONAL RESOURCES FOR THE STRATEGIC PLANNING PROCESS AVAILABLE FROM ASAE

Successful Association Leadership: Dimension of 21st Century Competency for the CEO (213552)
Getting Your Association Hooked on Quality: A How-to Guide and Workbook for CEO's, Volunteers, and Staff (218052)
Leading the Association: Striking the Right Balance Between Staff and Volunteers (213550)
Meeting the Change Challenge: The Executive's Guide to Leading Change in the Non-profit World (216726)
Managing Your Future as an Association: Thinking About Trends and Working With Their Consequences 1994-2020 (218055)
Keeping Members: The Myth and Realities (213551)
Associations and the Global Marketplace: Profiles of Success (216525)
Winning with Diversity: A Practical Handbook for Creating Inclusive Meetings, Events, and Organizations (218051)
Thriving in the Knowledge Age: A Survival Guide for your Association (218056)
Association Law Handbook, 3rd Edition (216465)

BENCHMARKING AND SURVEY REPORTS AVAILABLE FROM ASAE

ASAE Operating Ratio Report

Association Technology Trends

Association Meeting Trends

Association Executive Compensation and Benefits Study

Policies and Procedures in Association Management

The Association Insurance Program Guide and Survey Report

CONTACT ASAE AT 202-371-0940 FOR MORE INFORMATION.